With best wishes,
Jane Conner

LINCOLN IN STAFFORD

by Jane Hollenbeck Conner

"I am not concerned to know, if the Lord is on my side,
but whether I am on the Lord's side."
—A. Lincoln

ISBN 0-9708370-0-3
Parker Publishing, LLC
Stafford, Virginia

Designed by Ian Soper

Printed by Cardinal Press
Fredericksburg, Virginia

Contents

Acknowledgements

John Hennessy (Chief Historian of the Fredericksburg, Spotsylvania National Military Park Headquarters located at Chatham in Stafford County) first inspired me years ago with his fascinating talk about Lincoln during a Stafford County Historical Society meeting. After John heard I was writing a book about Lincoln, he generously let me copy the primary sources he had previously used for an article about the president. Throughout my work he answered numerous questions. Also at Chatham, with the National Park Service, are historians Eric Mink and Don Pfanz who generously took time to answer my questions and give helpful advice.

D.P. Newton and his dear mother, Polly, always welcomed me to the amazing *White Oak Civil War Museum and Research Center*. It was there that I spent days pouring through D.P's Corps Notebooks containing information about the troops in Stafford and copies of their letters. D.P. was generous in answering my endless questions. His deep knowledge led him to spend much time with his maps "taking me places" where Lincoln trod.

Ralph Gary in Texas, author of *In Lincoln's Footsteps,* was never too busy to correspond with me via e-mail. I appreciate his interest, even though it took him from his work on a new book.

My children, Michelle Porter and Doug Henderson, constantly had to listen to new facts I uncovered about the president. Doug joined me in traveling around the county locating sites of the various reviews and campsites, and Michelle helped me review the text.

My wonderful husband, Al Conner, answered unending questions during the past two years. His knowledge of the Civil War is truly remarkable. I so appreciate the time he spent in proofreading my text.

Introduction And Overview

The Civil War brought Lincoln to rural Stafford County, Virginia six different times for a total of fourteen days. This book describes these 1862 and 1863 visits as depicted in soldiers' letters, journals, newspaper articles, a war correspondent's notes, drawings, and photographs. It humanizes one of our greatest and most iconic presidents.

Lincoln made his first steamboat journeys to Stafford in April and May of 1862 during the federal occupation of Fredericksburg. He consulted with generals and visited with troops. In the winter, he was saddened to hear of the Union defeat at the Battle of Fredericksburg and the disastrous "Mud March" under General Burnside. He also heard that the over 130,000 troops were discouraged and forlorn. Besides being so demoralized, the soldiers were forced to spend their time in Stafford during a miserably cold winter causing one soldier to write, "This winter is, indeed the Valley Forge of the war."

In January of 1863, Lincoln changed the commander of the Army of the Potomac placing General Hooker in command. With better food, new clothing, and renewed discipline, the morale of the troops started to change.

In the spring, hearing from Hooker about the improved condition of the troops, Lincoln wanted to see the changes for himself and encourage the men. During his six day visit he reviewed over 60,000 men in one day; witnessed the largest cavalry review in the world; was kissed by a princess; and was accompanied by a world famous little person. While in Stafford, he spent time on horseback traveling from camp to camp. For hours he sat with wounded men in hospitals showing compassion and care. Soldiers in Stafford were inspired by his visit and wrote that their morale had improved.

Lincoln's next visit was April 19, 1863, the week before the Chancellorsville battle commenced. The president's final visit was in the aftermath of Hooker's Chancellorsville defeat.

The story ends with the election of 1864, in which Lincoln—with the undeniable aid of the army—defeated his rival, General George B. McClellan, and received the necessary mandate to continue the war effort to its fruition.

Prelude To Lincon's Visit

STAFFORD IN THE 1860S

Prior to the Civil War, Stafford was a shadow of its colonial prominence. Previously the county gave the nation an American president, a U.S. Supreme Court justice, two U.S. senators, two members of the U.S. Constitutional Convention, and three members of the Continental Congress. By the 1860s, Stafford had become a rather poor, rural, agricultural community with farms scattered throughout the county. The average farm consisted of 300 to 400 acres. Colonial tobacco plantations had given way to farming for subsistence and limited local commercial purposes.

Stafford's 1860 census population of 8,633 was small and surprisingly quite evenly split between whites and blacks (4,918 whites and 3,715 blacks). The black population included 321 free blacks and about ten times as many slaves, numbering 3,394. Slavery, however, was not as prevalent as the figures indicate, for out of 1,022 heads of white households in the county, 39% owned slaves. Most of those households owned fewer than five slaves. There were only two plantation owners with around 100 slaves each. Those were J. Horace Lacy of the Lacy House (Chatham) and Gustavus B. Wallace of Little Whim.[1]

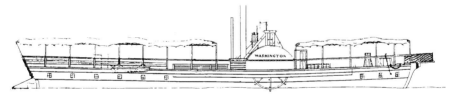

Daily steamship runs between Washington D.C. and Aquia Landing were established in 1815.
This 186-ton side paddle steamer "Washington" inaugurated the service.

For decades, the most common mode of land transportation in the county was horse or horse and wagon or stagecoach. If one wished to travel north it was a long journey which depended upon the weather, as the eastern Chopawamsic Creek area in northern Stafford became a swampy, muddy bog after rain and impeded traffic for weeks. The average trip from Richmond to Washington was thirty-eight hours in duration. The year 1815 brought forth a dramatic change with the emergence of the steamboat. Daily steamboat runs were established from Washington D.C. to Aquia Creek Landing. Aquia Landing became a busy port, as many travelers would disembark and catch a stagecoach and travel south to Richmond.

When the RF&P Railroad extended from Fredericksburg to Aquia Landing it cut down travel between Richmond and Washington D.C. to nine hours.

Twenty-seven years later, in 1842, another transportation change took place making Aquia Landing an important terminus. The RF&P Railroad (Richmond, Fredericksburg, and Potomac Railroad) laid track connecting Richmond to Aquia Landing. This cut the travel time from Washington to Richmond to 9 hours, consisting of a 3½ hour steamboat trip from Washington to Aquia Landing and then a 5½ trip aboard the RF&P to Richmond.[2]

START OF THE CIVIL WAR IN STAFFORD

1861

The Civil War began on April 12, 1861 with the southern, Confederate forces firing upon the Union-held Fort Sumter in South Carolina. Five days later, Virginia seceded from the Union. Naturally there were numerous Southern sympathizers in Stafford and many formed into units to defend Virginia. By the end of the war, around 1,000 Stafford men, or 41%, left their homes, leaving their families to fend for themselves.

On May 31, 1861, Stafford saw the first engagement of the Civil War between the U.S. Navy and the shore batteries of the Confederacy at Aquia Landing. Prior to that date, the Confederates believed that Union forces might attack via the Potomac, and if they got control of Aquia they could take over the RF&P Railroad. Therefore, the Confederates decided to set up artillery batteries, or groups of four to eight cannons, along the shore and in the hills surrounding the landing. Buoys and markers on the Potomac, near Aquia Landing, were removed by Confederates to disorient Union forces.

This drawing from *Frank Leslie's Illustrated Newspaper* shows action between Union ships and Confederate batteries at Aquia Landing in 1861.

Exchanges of fire continued through June 1st. Three Union ships, the USS *Thomas Freeborn*, USS *Anacostia*, and the USS *Resolute* were fired on by the Confederate shore batteries. The USS *Reliance* was also present but stayed out of range because it lacked rifled guns. The powerful Union ship, the USS *Pawnee*, also arrived mounting many guns. There was no decisive outcome. (The Southerners had a different take on the engagement. According to an article in *The Fredericksburg News*, dated June 4, 1861, "The 'Enemy" [was] in the shape of the Pawneee, Anacosta, Philadelphia, and James Guy...") The final result was reportedly limited to the death of a chicken and horse, the destruction of the wharf, and damage to part of the railroad tract and earthworks. Two of the Union ships were damaged. A reporter for the *Southern Christian Advocate* wrote of the battle, "If it takes six hours cannonading with near 600 rounds, from five steamers, to kill an old hen, how long before the South is conquered?"[3] From May 1861 to March 1862, Confederate troops from Virginia, Tennessee, Arkansas, North Carolina, Texas, and Georgia occupied Stafford. They protected the area from Federal forces and attempted to block Union shipping and travel along the Potomac.

Lincoln's First Visit To The Stafford Area

APRIL 19-20, 1862

For Abraham Lincoln, 1862 was a sad year. Not only was he concerned about the war and keeping the Union together, but in February his beloved third son, Willie, died of typhoid fever. This sorrow weighed heavily on his mind, but he remained, in today's rhetoric, a "hands-on" president. Daily, Lincoln would go to the War Department to hear and read the latest war news. Whenever able, he traveled to meet with officers and troops located near Washington.

A month after Willie's passing, Lincoln was informed that the Confederates began retreating from Stafford. By mid-April, 40,000 Union troops were occupying the area from Stafford Courthouse to Fredericksburg. Lincoln wished to go down to Aquia Landing to meet with General Irvin McDowell who was in charge of the occupying forces. The forces were blocking Confederate advance routes to Washington, D.C.

Each time Lincoln departed for Stafford, he left from the Washington Navy Yard in D.C.

On the cold, rainy Saturday afternoon of April 19th, 1862, Lincoln left the White House, traveled to the Washington Navy Yard, and boarded the steamer *Miami,* a revenue cutter 115 feet in-length and weighing 375 tons.[4] Accompanying him on the trip south to Aquia were five gentlemen, each an interesting and distinctive individual:

Edwin M. Stanton,
Secretary of War

In January, **Edwin M. Stanton**, a Democrat, had been appointed secretary of war by Lincoln. He left a successful law practice in Pittsburgh and Washington. Considered brusque and independent by many, Stanton at first mistrusted Lincoln but soon developed a great respect for him.

Salmon P. Chase,
Secretary of the Treasury

Salmon P. Chase, Lincoln's secretary of the treasury, had also been a practicing attorney. Unlike Stanton, he was a Republican. He agreed with Lincoln's anti-slavery views. Despite their similar political views, Lincoln found Chase cold and ambitious.

Commander John A.
Dahlgren, in charge of the
Washington Navy Yard

Commandant of the Navy Yard, **Commander John A. Dahlgren,** was also on board. This naval officer was a good friend of Lincoln. Lincoln frequently visited him at the Navy Yard and examined new weapons being demonstrated. Dahlgren biographer Robert Schneller relates that while Lincoln and Dahlgren delighted in being with one another, they had widely different personalities. Lincoln was always quick with a joke and always ready to poke fun at himself, while Dahlgren was neither a back-slapper nor jokester.[5]

Ulric Dahlgren,
son of the Commander

Called "Ully" by his father, **Ulric Dahlgren**, was also aboard. Father and son were often visitors at the White House. Ully received a commission from Stanton about a month after this trip. On May 29, 1862, at twenty years of age, he became an aide-de-camp with the rank of captain.

D. Dudley Field,
a New York lawyer

D. Dudley Field was a well-known New York attorney who had developed a legal reform system adopted in twenty-four states. Originally a Democrat, Field opposed the party's proslavery policy. During the Civil War he was a staunch supporter of the president and actively wrote and spoke in favor of the administration and gave money to aid his country. Why he was onboard the *Miami* is unknown. Possibly he happened to be at the White House and was asked by the president to accompany him.

After an almost four-hour trip, Lincoln and party reached Aquia Landing before dark. They observed the recently abandoned and burned wharf. The railroad track, reconstructed after the 1861 naval skirmish, had been destroyed again by the departing southern forces. Abandoned, too, were the Confederate batteries that previously dotted the shore. Commander Dahlgren sent ashore for a senior officer. Finding the officer knew "nothing," a *Herald* reporter was picked up who Dahlgren said, "knew everything." After interviewing the reporter, Dahlgren sent men ashore to find McDowell for the president. Realizing McDowell would be there in the morning, the gentlemen spent the night aboard the cutter. Dahlgren recalled that they had a wonderful evening in a little cabin listening to the president tell jokes. One was:

> The school was very noisy, and one of the most uproarious had been called up by the teacher to be disciplined. "Hold out your hand!" A paw of the most surprising description was extended, more remarkable for its filthiness than anything else. The astonished schoolmaster gazed silently with suspended ferule [cane] at the uncleanly spectacle. "Now, if there were such another dirty thing in the room, I would let you off." "There it is," quoth the unmoved culprit, drawing the other hand from behind his back and presenting it to the petrified dominie [master].[6]

The U.S. Revenue Cutter Miami carried the Presidential party from Washington, D.C. to Aquia Landing.

Lincoln, Secretary of Treasury Chase, and Secretary of War Stanton conferred aboard the *Miami*.

On the 20th, morning sunlight peeked through the rain and brought forth General Irvin McDowell. McDowell had, as one reporter wrote, a "square full face and commanding figure."[7] After congratulations were given to McDowell for occupying Fredericksburg, it was then decided that McDowell should return with them to Washington. They left Aquia at 8:00 a.m. and en route discussed the number of men available for McDowell and other commanders. Evidently, they also discussed the possibility of McDowell's men moving straight down to Richmond. It rained during the entire return journey to D.C. Arriving at the Navy Yard at 2:30 p.m. the party went straight to Dahlgren's home on base to dine. After eating, each man departed for home. However, the trip from the Washington Naval Yard to the White House was adventurous for the president. Excited horses which pulled his carriage were immobilized, so the trip required another carriage. That night, despite a long and busy day, the president met with a senator to discuss the Yorktown, Virginia and Corinth, Mississippi battles.[8] Regardless of the hour, the President was always interested in his troops and their progress.

Between Visits

RECONSTRUCTION IN STAFFORD

Herman Haupt

General Irvin Mc Dowell

After viewing the destruction at Stafford's Aquia Landing and hearing that all the railroad bridges had been destroyed, Secretary of War Stanton contacted the highly regarded railroad engineer and mechanical genius Herman Haupt. He requested that Haupt, then in Boston, promptly report to Washington. Stanton added that General McDowell had been asked to move his troops and supplies south but was unable to do so because of the destruction.[9]

Haupt promptly traveled to Washington, conferred with Stanton, and traveled south to Belle Plain to meet with McDowell. (Belle Plain, located on Potomac Creek, was a landing south of Aquia. It was at the end of today's Belle Plains Road. During the Civil War soldiers called it Belle Plain. Today it is known as Belle Plains.) Coincidentally, Haupt realized that he and McDowell had met at West Point as cadets.

Haupt returned to Washington and was officially designated a chief of construction and transportation for the U.S. Military Railroads. He was given the rank of colonel and appointed aide-de-camp on McDowell's staff. Haupt immediately traveled to Aquia Landing and started reconstructing the burned one-acre wharf, repairing three miles of destroyed track, and replacing missing rails and burned ties.[10]

For this construction, Haupt was given soldiers who lacked experience to accomplish the rebuilding of the wharf, the railroad track, and bridges. On the other hand, intelligent young officers from surrounding units were used as assistant engineers. Soldiers cut and split trees in the nearby woods creating over 3,000 cross ties. Lacking normal tools and railroad construction experience, they leveled the track beds with sticks. Rain and mud hindered their work. Nevertheless, the soldiers worked through the wet nights using lanterns and remarkably laid three miles of track in three days.[11]

The bridge over Accokeek Creek had to be rebuilt. (It was located where today's Brooke Road crosses over Accokeek Creek.) The span was almost 150 feet wide, and the bridge would have to reach an elevation of 30 feet above the water. The bridge was erected in an amazing fifteen hours; shortly thereafter, McDowell rode across the bridge on a railroad engine.[12]

Haupt thought it was remarkable that this Potomac Creek Bridge, built in nine days for foot travel, was constructed by common soldiers and not mechanics. Eventually, the bridge carried trains once an hour.

The bridge across the Potomac Creek was a greater challenge, as the deep chasm was 400 feet wide. The bridge would have to reach 80 feet in elevation. Logs were cut in the woods, but only a few were adequate for crib foundations. Help arrived in the form of soldiers, some of whom were lumberjacks from Wisconsin and Indiana Regiments. However, out of 100-120 men, many were sickly and few were willing to climb the poles and ropes at high elevation. Nevertheless, the bridge was completed in nine days for foot travel, and in less than two weeks for engine travel. The bridge required over two million feet of lumber. Haupt later wrote, "The most remarkable feature about this bridge is the fact that it was built by common soldiers, not by mechanics."[13] (The bridge was located at the east end of today's Route 625.)

Lincoln's Second Visit

POETRY, WASHINGTON,
AND FREDERICKSBURG

May 22-23, 1862

Lincoln left Washington on May 22nd for an overnight trip down the Potomac to Stafford. Accompanying him again were Secretary of War Stanton and Commander Dahlgren. Dahlgren was telegraphed by Stanton that he wished to travel to Aquia Landing that evening but failed to mention Lincoln joining them. Therefore, the commander was surprised when Lincoln's carriage arrived at the Naval Yard. Apparently, only Mrs. Lincoln knew the president was accompanying them. Dahlgren remembered, "I told them there was nothing to eat in the steamboat. I had eatables, bedding, &c., tumbled in, and we left at ten P.M., after supper."[14]

Underway, the president read poetry aloud to the two gentlemen. Evidently, when Lincoln read, he read with pathos and feeling. That evening he read Fritz-Greene Halleck's poem, *Marco Bozzaris.* Ironically, part of the poem would prove prophetic for Lincoln :

> For thou art Freedom's now, and Fame's;
> One of the few, the immortal names,
> That were not born to die.[15]

The Potomac Creek Bridge was dubbed the *Beanpoles and Cornstalks Bridge* by Lincoln.
Lincoln even walked across this engineering wonder on a plank-wide path in 1862.

The next morning the steamer was anchored by Aquia Landing, while Lincoln, Stanton, and Dahlgren waited for a railroad car. They finally boarded a baggage car equipped with camp stools and traveled over the rebuilt railroad track. When they reached the trestle bridge over Potomac Creek, General McDowell was waiting for them and pointed out the recently created master-piece. Boyishly, Lincoln suggested that the party walk over it. Although the pathway was a mere plank wide, the president led the way. Halfway across Stanton became dizzy, so Dahlgren, although dizzy himself, helped the secretary across.[16] (Later in Washington Lincoln recalled, "…the most remarkable structure that human eyes ever rested upon. That man Haupt has built a bridge across Potomac Creek, about 400 feet long and nearly 100 feet high, over which loaded trains are running every hour, and upon my word, gentlemen, there is nothing in it but beanpoles and cornstalks."[17])

Lincoln departed the train at Falmouth Station. It was located approximately where the Eagles Lodge on Cool Springs Road is today.

After an adventurous journey across the bridge, the president's party re-boarded the train and traveled to Falmouth Railroad Station. (The station was located near the corner of Cool Springs Road and Route 218, approximately at the site of today's Fraternal Order of Eagles Lodge.) Falmouth Station consisted of a warehouse, a platform, quartermaster tents, and several sidings.[18] There, the party boarded a carriage and traveled to the nearby Lacy House, McDowell's headquarters. (Now and originally known as Chatham, the house is located off Chatham Heights Road.) The Lacy House was a lovely Colonial brick mansion on the bluffs overlooking the Rappahannock River and the town of Fredericksburg. After breakfast, Lincoln was visited by civilian leaders and conferred with brigade commanders.

Later, McDowell took Lincoln and Stanton by carriage to George Washington's boyhood home, known today as Ferry Farm. (Route 3, about a mile east of Chatham Bridge) No doubt, Lincoln was thrilled at the prospect of being on the grounds where Washington, whom he so greatly admired, grew up. Once he expressed his feelings about the first president by saying:

> Washington is the mightiest name of earth—long since mightest in the cause of civil liberty…To add brightness to the sun, or glory to the name of Washington, is alike impossible. Let none attempt it.[19]

 Growing up, one of Lincoln's favorite books was Parson Weems's biography of Washington, which told of the fabled cherry tree incident. Historian William C. Davis said that, "Weems left an impression of the meaning of freedom and sacrifice and citizenship on young Lincoln."[20] Lincoln even referred to the book during a February 1861 speech:

> May I be pardoned if, upon this occasion, I mention that away back in my childhood, the earliest days of my being able to read, I got hold of a small book… Weems's *Life of Washington.* I remember all the accounts there given of the battle fields and struggles for the liberties of the country.[21]

A carriage carrying the president passed over George Washington's farm and then over the Rappahannock River on this canal-boat bridge.

Lincoln's carriage, pulled by four iron-gray horses, passed over the Washington grounds and to the Rappahannock River.[22] Built there was canal-boat bridge. Twenty days earlier, Betty Herndon Maury of Fredericksburg wrote about the construction of the bridge in her diary:

> Went down yesterday evening to see the bridge of canal boats that the Yankees are building at the lower wharf. The boats are laid close together side by side. The length of the boat being the width of the bridge. Eight boats are in place and it already reaches more than half way across the river.[23]

Marsena Patrick escorted Lincoln throughout the town of Fredericksburg.

Once the carriage traveled across the bridge into Fredericksburg, they were greeted by General Marsena Patrick who was commanding Union troops in town. He already met the president at the Lacy House earlier that morning. Patrick led the cortege through Fredericksburg. The president visited Patrick's troops and then went to Patrick's headquarters, the Farmer's Bank. (Today known as The National Bank of Fredericksburg, it is located at the corner of

Princess Anne and George Streets.) According to Patrick's diary they remained in the building for half an hour.[24] John Tackett Goolrick, a young man at the time and later a local attorney and judge, recalled hearing the President make a speech after leaving the bank:

> …President Lincoln from the front steps made a short but splendid address. The writer of this, sat on the steps of the St. George's Church, on the opposite side of the street and heard President Lincoln's speech.[25]

Lincoln and Patrick stayed a half hour in the Farmer's Bank. Afterwards Lincoln gave a speech from the bank's steps.

Lincoln and party, still accompanied by Patrick, departed town and reviewed a division. The president rode along the lines with his hat off while Union soldiers cheered. Undoubtedly, Confederate sympathizers stayed in their homes peeking out windows to secretly view this "Yankee" president. General Patrick escorted the presidential carriage to the bridge and said, "Adieu" as the party crossed the Rappahannock River into Stafford.

Returning to the Lacy House, Lincoln discovered that French Minister Mercier and Admiral Julien de la Graviere had arrived from Washington. After a brief rest, the President and the Frenchmen reviewed nearby divisions on horseback. In his memoir, Dahlgren mentioned that Secretary Stanton could not mount a horse because of an old knee injury, so the two of them rode in an ambulance and followed the others. (An ambulance was a vehicle with two axles and springs.) Dahlgren feared Lincoln would be "hurt by the sun" as he reviewed the troops bare-headed. Dahlgren also wrote that they reviewed so many cheering troops that he felt they had traveled ten miles.[26]

The Lacy House (Chatham) was headquarters for General McDowell. It was here where Lincoln conferred with generals and ate breakfast and lunch.

Finally, after the exhausting afternoon, the Lincoln party returned to the Lacy House at 6:00 p.m. and sat down to dinner (what we would call lunch) in the mansion's dining room. One of McDowell's staff officers wrote that there were fourteen present: "I Prest, I Secy, I foreign minister, I admiral and his aid, I commodore, 3 Maj. Genls, 3 Brigr, and 2 Colonels. The line had to be drawn somewhere, and they could not go below a colonel!"[27]

At 9:00 p.m. they departed by railroad train at Falmouth Station, arriving at Aquia Landing for a 10 p.m. departure to Washington. Mercier took a tug boat on which he had arrived. The president was in good spirits, and they all sat down to supper aboard the steamer. Afterwards, Lincoln again read Halleck's poems aloud, and the party went to bed. The steamship arrived at the Navy Yard at 3:00 a.m.; however, Lincoln did not rise until 5:00 a.m. Dahlgren wrote, "The President came in from his room half dressed, and sat down between the Secretary and myself. He was reminded of a joke, at which we laughed heartily."[28] Early that morning, after leaving the Navy Yard, the President visited the War Department. His unending concern about the troops and their movements was tremendously admirable.

Prior To And During Lincoln's Third Visit

CHANGES CONTINUE IN STAFFORD

November, 1862

After Lincoln's departure from Stafford, Herman Haupt converted Aquia Landing into, as historian Homer Musselman states, "a small city of offices, warehouses, and shops. Haupt built storage facilities at Brooke, Stoneman's Switch [off today's Leeland Road, north of Leeland Station] and Falmouth to unload the cars." Mechanics devised unique ways to transport loaded railroad cars via converted barges. Entire loaded cars could be unloaded directly from the water onto the tracks via floating wharves.[29]

Loaded railroad cars from ports like Alexandria would be placed on barges and shipped south to Aquia Landing. From there they would be unloaded onto railroad tracks on floating whaves.

In the fall of 1862, Union officers worried that Confederates would attack Washington. All the Federals would be needed to protect the capital city. This meant the Union forces would leave Fredericksburg and Stafford. Not wanting the Confederates to use Aquia Landing and all the new facilities, fifty-seven boxcars were rolled onto the pier and set on fire. Even the bridges, including Lincoln's beanpoles and cornstalk bridge, were destroyed. Destruction of facilities went all the way down the railroad track to Falmouth. A Fredericksburg resident was quoted in a *Richmond Dispatch* article dated September 5, 1862:

> The last few days our city has been in considerable excitement after being subjected to over four months of Yankee despotism…when the city was evacuated, large columns of smoke began to immediately rise opposite our city from Falmouth; occasioned by their burning of some buildings they had occupied in Falmouth and their commissary stores opposite us to the amount of $500,000 to $1,000,000.

Meanwhile, in Maryland, just twelve days after this article was printed, the Battle of Antietam took place, which included the "bloodiest single day of the war." Both the Union and the Confederacy lost over 2,000 men and each had over 9,000 wounded. No distinct winner emerged. General George McClellan, in command of the Army of the Potomac (a force of 75-87,000 men), complained and blamed others despite outnumbering Lee's troops by 24,000 men. Lincoln, displeased with McClellan's actions, felt the general had thrown away a chance to win the war. Lincoln traveled to Maryland to meet with McClellan and visit the army. During his visit he concealed his opinion of the general and rode with him on horseback to visit the camps.

Lincoln frequently reviewed the troops. He is shown here at Sharpsburg, Maryland speaking to General McClellan.

The next month, Herman Haupt received a message from McClellan that his troops would be returning to Stafford and needed Haupt to reestablish the wharves at Aquia and rebuild the railroad bridges. Needless to say, Haupt was less than pleased and responded:

> The destruction of this road was an unfortunate piece of vandalism on the part of our troops. I reported to General Halleck that the destruction of this road was unnecessary and highly censurable…The wharf at Aquia Creek was a very complete affair, covering an area of nearly an acre and a half, with double tracks and commodious buildings. It cannot be reconstructed as it was in four months."[30]

Major General Ambose Burnside took over the command of the Army of the Potomac from General McClellan.

On November 5, 1862, Lincoln relieved General McClellan of command and appointed General Ambrose Burnside as commander of the Army of the Potomac. McClellan, or "Little Mac" as the troops called him, was much loved by his men. He was cheered by his troops during his last review; however, they felt as if they were attending a funeral. Lincoln's decision angered them, and some officers even resigned their commissions.[31] Others openly spoke of mutiny.

Burnside, McClellan's replacement, was a strapping six-footer with well known whiskers, dubbed "sideburns." He pleaded with Lincoln twice before that he did not wish to take command. Burnside was ordered to take command, so he reluctantly accepted.

Like McClellan, Burnside planned to go through Stafford and Fredericksburg on his way to capture Richmond. He would be bringing with him over 115,000 men from Warrenton, Virginia. This necessitated Haupt to order reconstruction in Stafford. In the middle of November he requisitioned barges, pile drivers, pile scows, boats, anchors, timber and other necessary materials for rebuilding. Fortunately, not all of the wharf at Aquia Landing had been destroyed, so by November 27th Haupt accomplished the impossible; the wharf was repaired and trains were running all the way from Aquia Landing to Falmouth.

THE YANKEES ARE COMING, THE YANKEES ARE COMING

November, 1862

Aquia Landing started to grow as Union troops flowed into Stafford.

Eventually over 135,000 Union troops swarmed into Stafford, making it the largest encampment in United States military history. A member of the 5th New Hampshire Regiment wrote that the Army of the Potomac moved into the county and consumed every piece of wood in constructing shelters, cooking food, staying warm, and constructing roads:

> This vast army…pushing out, and out and out, through field and forest, swept over the country…Fences and forage, mules and horses, hogs, cattle and fowls disappeared before this moving monster. Compact, elastic, winding in and out through a wood, over a stream, around a bog, through swamp, with feelers in every direction, they pushed into every dwelling and barn, down into every well, up into every loft, and through every smokehouse and spring-house. On they pushed, covered with dust or mud, many foot sore…

Camps sprang up throughout Stafford to house the large Army of the Potomac. These troops from Pennsylvania are visiting with a chaplain in the tall hat.

The Army of the Potomac settled throughout Stafford, covering more than 200 square miles. Camps sprung up everywhere consisting of various types of shelters. One Union soldier wrote to his mother describing his dwelling, a very common type of shelter:

> Three of us have, by digging about 4 feet into the ground and raising it 6 log's high, then using our shelter tent for roofing, made quite comfortable quarters. We have got a bunk made of poles covered with cedar boughs in the place of feathers, in one end. In the other a regular old fashioned fire place. Some men dug out steep banks and still others made their shelters out of small logs. Most were about eight by ten

feet in size and about five feet high. Spaces between the logs were plastered with mud. Hillsides made good fireplaces. Many shelters were finished with stone and had stick and mud chimneys, while some used barrels for chimneys.

Others had "sugar loaf" tents or "Sibley" tents. Looking like an Indian teepee, these tents were also shaped like sugar cones. A kettle for cooking and heating would hang in the center. Smoke would rise through a hole in the peak. Unfortunately, these canvas tents would sometimes burn or get so heavy with snow and collapse "like a pancake" under the weight.

This drawing by Edwin Forbes shows various types of shelters that were constructed in the county.

The consumption of the land and its products by this huge army left one member of the Union's III Corps to write, "the country looks as if a grasshopper would have to handle himself pretty lively to find enough grass to survive."

THE BATTLE OF FREDERICKSBURG DELAYED

November, 1862

Burnside wanted a frontal attack on the Confederates at Fredericksburg. He positioned most of the Army of the Potomac opposite Fredericksburg on Stafford Heights and as far north as Stafford Courthouse. Burnside had expected to cross the 400 foot wide expanse of the river via floating pontoon bridges. While in Warrenton, Virginia, he discovered that these massive 31 foot long and 5 foot wide pontoon boats were up in Berlin, Maryland, near Harper's Ferry, and in Washington, DC. Therefore, he requested the pontoon trains, consisting of the boats, special wagons, horses, and teamsters, be shipped to Stafford. Burnside hoped they would arrive about the same time as he and his troops.

Burnside waited for pontoon boats, like these, to arrive before he would cross the Rappahannock.

Unfortunately for General Burnside, poor weather, misunderstood orders, bad planning, and communications delayed the trains' journey. After leaving Maryland, the boats had a fifty mile journey via the C&O Canal down to Washington. Once there, the pontoon boats were divided into two groups. One group of boats would go via water and another via land.

The forty-eight boats of the water route were lashed together and towed down the Potomac by steamboat. Unfortunately, the steamer got stuck on a sandbar just outside of Washington. Regardless of this delay, this group of boats arrived at Aquia Landing on November 18th, a day after the Army of the Potomac entered Stafford.

Meanwhile, the land group, consisting of dozens of wagons, 270 horses, pontoons, and many teamsters, was struggling. When the horses arrived, they were unbroken for harness, further delaying the train. This pontoon train also toiled through rain. Upon reaching the Occoquan River they discovered it was swollen. Rather than continue, fifty-eight pontoon boats were lashed together and sent down the Potomac much like the water group. The horses, men, and wagons slowly continued via land and finally reached Aquia Landing on November 25th.

Finally, after a long delay, pontoon trains were brought from Aquia Landing to Stafford Heights.

LINCOLN'S THIRD VISIT
TO THE STAFFORD AREA

November 26-27, 1862

In Washington on the 25th, at 11:30 a.m., Lincoln sent a message to General Burnside at the Phillips House. "If I should be in a Boat off Aquia-Creek, at dark to-morrow ([W]ednesday) evening, could you, without inconvenience, meet me & pass an hour or two with me?"[32] Burnside replied at 2:45 p.m., "I will meet you, as you request, to-morrow evening. Please inform me what boat you will be on."[33]

Wednesday evening the president left Washington on the steamer, *Baltimore*. (This side wheeler had previously been captured from the Confederates. It measured 200 feet in length and weighed 500 tons.[34]) Supposedly, neither General in Chief Halleck nor Secretary of War Stanton knew that Lincoln was departing for Stafford. Some historians say that Lincoln ended up at Belle Plain Landing rather than Aquia Landing. In any event, on Thursday, Lincoln and Burnside conferred on the *Baltimore* at Aquia Landing and discussed the taking of Fredericksburg which was now controlled by the Confederate forces. Lincoln returned to Washington before noon.[35]

General Burnside received a message from Lincoln at the Phillips House.

Winter Disasters And Triumphs

THE BATTLE OF FREDERICKSBURG

December 11-15, 1862

Almost a month had passed since Burnside first arrived with his army on November 17th. Ironically, had he immediately crossed the Rappahannock River where it narrows at Falmouth, without the aid of pontoon bridges, he might easily have trapped Confederate General Robert E. Lee's 1,000 troops in Fredericksburg, as Lee did not yet have all his men in place. While Burnside had waited weeks for the pontoon trains to arrive, Lee's experienced generals, "Stonewall" Jackson and James Longstreet, moved their corps securely into position. The Confederate force now consisted of 78,000 men. They were waiting for the Federal attack. Many troops were entrenched in the heights behind the city and were in an unassailable position on the Sunken Road behind a stone wall. One Confederate cannoneer said, "A chicken could not live on that field when we open on it."

Some scholars argue that Burnside knew what was taking place on the other side of the river and lacked the mental agility to change his plans. Burnside had a limited chance to succeed but attempted to cross the Rappahannock on December 11th. By the 13th, the Federal troops attacked the Confederates troops despite the fact that their enemy occupied an elevated position with clear fields of fire across an open area. The Union suffered 12,653 casualties (killed, wounded, captured, or missing). Half that number, 4,576, were Confederates casualties–a staggering difference of 8,077!

A corporal wrote of the Union troops' utter despair. "Since the Battle of Fredericksburg some of the soldiers of the old regiments have been wandering around not knowing where their companies are. Some of them don't want to find their regiments. They curse the union and the administration to the depths of hell."[36]

Virtually all of the Union soldiers were devastated after the loss at Fredericksburg. Bitter feelings were intensified when troops realized that Christmas parties were being held at various headquarters. Officers dined on turkey, chicken, roast beef, and ham, accompanied with liquors, while common soldiers ate hardtack and salt pork.[37]

Troops disliked the cold winter in Stafford. One referred to it as the "Valley Forge of the War."

A letter written on Christmas Day by a Wisconsin soldier camped near Belle Plain said, "This army seems to be overburdened with second rate men in high positions, from General Burnside down...This winter is, indeed, the Valley Forge of the war."

EMANCIPATION PROCLAMATION

January 1, 1863

Early in the morning on New Year's Day, 1863, President Lincoln held a three hour reception at the White House. Following the reception, he went upstairs to sign the Emancipation Proclamation. He said that his hands were shaking so much, but then realized that it was not because of the fear of signing the proclamation, but because he had previously been shaking hands for so many hours. Chuckling to himself he signed the proclamation stating that "all persons held as slaves" within the rebellious states "shall be then, thenceforward, and forever free." He said, "I never in my life, felt more certain that I was doing right than I do in signing this paper." Usually he just signed his correspondence "A. Lincoln," but for this historic signing, he wrote, "Abraham Lincoln." He prophetically added, "If my name ever goes into history, it will be for this act."[38] Later he said of the proclamation, "The moment came when I felt that slavery must die that the nation might live."[39]

Lincoln and his cabinet adopted the Emancipation Proclamation in September of 1862, but it was officially signed on January 1st of 1863.

Meanwhile, down in Stafford, troops were receiving the news. The reviews of Lincoln's latest action were mixed. Some Northerners felt like freedom for the slaves should have happened before and were very pleased. Others were worried, for the proclamation also stated that the freed slaves could join the Federal forces. They did not know if they could work side by side with them. Still others were angry. One soldier from Indiana wrote a letter home from Belle Plain on January 9th:

> This grand army is the worst demoralized it ever was. The boys all say…they never come here to free the negroes. At best, I had thoughts of fighting for anything only the restoration of the union, which might have been done before this late hour if our Generals had not worked against each other for the sake of honor, the Generals wate for that Abolition President and War department.[40]

THE MUD MARCH

January 20–21, 1863

For several cold, winter weeks after the Battle of Fredericksburg, the two armies remained on the Rappahannock's opposite shores while caring for their injured and burying their dead. General Burnside then conceived a plan to move the Federal forces upstream and launch an attack on the Confederates. (Today that would mean moving from Chatham and Falmouth, along the Rappahannock shoreline, and west on Highway 17 toward Geico.) He wished to cross the river at Banks Ford to attack General Robert E. Lee's left flank. (Banks Ford is near the present-day site of Celebrate Virginia's golf course, Cannon Ridge.)

On January 14, 1863, soldiers were told to get ready for a six mile march, as the roads were in good condition and the weather after the Battle of Fredericksburg was favorable. The men were ordered to dispose of camp furniture. It was thought that they could travel better without surplus baggage. This meant that ingeniously constructed furniture made from the bark and roots of trees had to be destroyed along with bread boxes and barrels that had been made into chairs, desks, and trunks. Abandoned, too, were dice, chessmen, and checkerboards. One soldier from the 16th Maine Regiment cleverly dug a grave and put in his treasures and marked it with a headboard. A cook even buried his favorite frying pan. Some officers told their men to destroy shelters, for they would not be returning. However, on the 15th, because of a heavy storm, orders to move were countermanded and troops remained in their camps.

Icy rains fell down upon the troops for three days.

Four days later, on January 19th and 20th, orders were again issued to pack up and march out of the camps. A soldier wrote that "…trumpets sounded, drums beat, whips cracked and mules squealed and teamsters cursed." Columns were put in motion parallel to the river. During the night of the 20th a terrible storm came up. A letter written by a member of the Iron Brigade to his sister sums up the three days of icy rain that had turned the roads into bottomless pits.

> …it rained hard all night…at 9 oclock in the morning we started again. raining hard all the time. We marched until about 4 and found all the army ahead of us stuck in the mud raining some yet. we stopt there all night all the next day and next night. on the morning of the 23rd we started on the back track mud about knee deep some of the way. Every hollar that we came to we would find 2 or 3 wagons stuck fast.

Even pontoon wagons got stuck in the mud. Reportedly, 150 men would try in vain to move just one. Guns normally pulled by six-horse teams would stay rooted in the mud even with twelve-horse teams. When a horse or mule would collapse in the mud it would be cut from its harness and be left behind to perish. The futility of the march was expressed by an officer's comedic request for "50 men, 25 feet high, to work in mud 18 feet deep."[41] Another soldier wrote:

> I don't know how the world's surface looked after the flood in Noah's time, but I am certain it could not have appeared more saturated than does the present surface of the Old Dominion."[42]

Wagons, pontoon boats, animals, artillery, and men were bogged down in the fathomless mud.

Realizing that the troops could go no farther, Burnside abandoned his plan to cross the river, and the men returned slowly through the mud to their original camps. Some soldiers sang "Burnside's Army lies floundering in the mud," to the tune of *John Brown's Body* as they attempted to march back through the mire. Those units which did not destroy their quarters were delighted to "get back home." However, many were not quite as fortunate. A member of the 13th Massachusetts Volunteers wrote:

> We found the camp in sorry condition, from the rain and the disorder in which we left it. Those of us who destroyed our huts when we left this spot on the 20th felt badly enough as we gazed on the ruins.

A member of the New York Volunteers wrote to his uncle after the Mud March and said, "It rained all last night and to cap the climax, it is snowing today. Will Ure says he would be satisfied if he only had as good quarters as your hog pen would make."

A soldier, writing to the *Springfield Republican,* discussed the troops:

> Talk about demoralization of the Army! Well, we have fallen pretty low. We haven't the same strain of lofty patriotism in our talk as when we first came out. We have been knocked round and starved and frozen...[43]

A description of the Falmouth area by a member of the 5th New Hampshire depicts the awful sights and smells that were encountered by the discouraged troops:

> Acres of land were covered with dead horses and mules, scattered about in convenient groups. Their bloating, decaying, festering bodies filled the air with an intolerable stench, and afforded a disgusting feast to the thousands of buzzards which gorged themselves until unable to fly or walk...

Horses, mules, wagons, and cannons were abandoned in the mud as troops returned to their old quarters.

A NEW LEADER

"Fighting Joe Hooker"

On January 25th, a day after the disastrous Mud March, Burnside was relieved of duty. Lincoln ordered General Joseph Hooker to take command of the Army of the Potomac. Hooker was, as many described, a handsome, dashing soldier. This West Point graduate had wavy blond hair, blue eyes, and a rosy complexion. He was nicknamed "Fighting Joe Hooker" for showing bravery at the battle at Antietam. Despite being shot in the foot, he remained in his saddle and fought with his men.

General Hooker became the new commander of the Army of the Potomac

After Hooker took command, Lincoln wrote the general a now famous letter and ended it by stating, "And now, beware of rashness. Beware of rashness, but with energy, and sleepless vigilance, go forward, and give us victories."

At the end of January, Hooker wanted to completely overhaul the Army of the Potomac, for there were 3,000 officers and 82,000 enlisted men reported absent. Some were sick, wounded or on furlough, but most were just not answering roll call. Many had run away, with approximately 200 desertions a day.[44]

Even though this photograph is identified as being a bakery at Stoneman's Switch in Stafford County, it is actually a bakery in Alexandria. Bakeries were sprinkled throughout Stafford under the direction of Hooker. Fresh bread was a wonderful treat for the soldiers.

Immediately, General Hooker took positive measures to transform the Army of the Potomac. He ordered changes in the equipment and discipline of the troops with scheduled drills. Marksmanship was stressed and hundreds of rifle ranges were spread throughout the area. Food was improved. Rations of fresh beef were issued. Bakeries were established, so fresh bread could replace hardtack. Fresh vegetables gave greater variety to a hungry army. New equipment, clothing, and shoes were distributed. One soldier wrote, "We looked and felt much better in our new uniforms."[45]

This picture of General Whipple's headquarters in Falmouth shows how pine boughs were used for decoration.

Burnside had organized the army into four grand divisions of two corps each. Hooker eliminated the grand divisions and divided the army into eight corps of approximately 10,000–20,000 men. He gave each its own corps badge, an idea suggested by General Butterfield, his chief of staff. The idea proved popular with both officers and troops. Each corps restored its own camp, or neighborhood, in Stafford. Most constructed their shelters in rows or streets. Camp streets were named and some were decorated with pine boughs and distinctive badges. Eventually pride was reemerging.

This distant view of Aquia Creek Landing by Alexander Gardner shows the growth of the landing to support the 135,000 men of the Army of the Potomac.

Aquia Landing became a major receiving and distribution center for the Union.

Large structures were constructed at Aquia Landing. Here personnel line up in front of the Quartermaster's office.

The railroad was important in getting supplies to the many soldiers. Here commissary clerks stand by goods at Aquia Landing.

By February 1863, Aquia Landing was a major, busy port again. A Pennsylvania corporal wrote to his mother from a camp overlooking Aquia Landing:

> I can see for miles up and down the Potomac. Vessels coming and going, under full sail and others with a full head of steam driving ahead, giving an occasional puff of their whistle. All bustle and confusion about the landing as the 9th Army Corps is going out on transports for Fortress Monroe or New Bern. See a steamboat back out with a band playing and colors flying, its grand I tell you. And then again the Rail Road passes just in stones throw from our camp, the Locomotive screeching and puffing. Trains loaded with soldiers, both going and coming. All this work going on…[46]

Despite the winter cold, Federal troops were beginning to enjoy life again. For example, in February near Belle Plain, it was reported that the "boys" lined the streets with snowballs and were ready to throw at the first "shoulder-strap" (officer) that they would find. Sometimes they would divide a company (50-100 men) into two groups and delight themselves by having snowball fights using military terms such as "flanked" and "attacked in the rear." The soldiers also placed a bass drum at a distance and took pleasure when it would be hit.

Also in February, a soldier wrote from Camp Pitcher (near the present day Conway Elementary School) describing how the troops celebrated a special holiday:

> It commence snowing about dark last night & when we got up this morning we found a pyramid of snow about three feet high in one corner of the tent. And an extra blanket of the same material covering our persons. The snow is deepest I remember to have seen it for several years. Washingtons birth day was celebrated by a salute of thirty four guns fired from different batteries in the neighborhood.

This drawing by Edwin Forbes shows the wonderful time had by all at a St. Patrick's Day celebration in the spring of 1863.

St. Patrick's Day was celebrated by the Irish Brigade in Falmouth. For days they prepared a race track and field and even sent out advertisements for the event. On March 17th, they had a horse race and hurdle jumping featuring man-made lakes. Beside those events there were mule, foot, and sack racing, picking up stones, and climbing a greased pole. The quartermaster sent to Washington for supplies for a banquet which followed the events. According to a history of the Irish Brigade, the fare consisted of:

> Thirty-five hams, and a side of an ox roasted; an entire pig stuffed with boiled turkeys; an unlimited number of chickens, ducks and small game. The drinking materials comprised eight baskets of champagne, ten gallons of rum, and twenty-two of whiskey.[47]

Bell Air was located nearby today's Conway Elementary. The home was, at one time, the headquarters of General Birney. Shown here is the back of the house.

There was another horse race on March 28th. According to a Massachusetts soldier, this horse race celebration was "…similar to but on a more extended scale than those which celebrated St. Patrick's Day in the Irish Brigade."[48] This one was located by General Birney's headquarters, Bell Air, a two and a half story frame house with a full-length porch decorated with evergreens (today near the site of Conway School, former Walnut Farms). A reviewing stand, 120 feet long and 16 feet in depth, was filled with, "a large number of army officers from the different corps, and many distinguished statesmen, civilians and lady visitors from the North."[49] According to soldiers' letters there were at least fifty women in brightly colored dresses. One soldier described them as, "Real women, be-silked, be-furred, and bonneted…"[50] General Hooker and Governor Andrew Curtin of Pennsylvania were two of the dignitaries present. After the horse races, hurdle jumping, foot races, sack races and greased pole climbing, there was an "Ethiopian Concert" or minstrel show.[51]

The weather also contributed to raising the spirits of the men. When spring appeared grass began to grow on muddy fields. Birds returned to the area. Troops were "abundantly supplied with fresh fish, chiefly shad, rock and herring, of admirable size and quality from the government fisheries at Aquia Creek."[52]

General Darius Couch wrote of the results of Hooker's remarkable changes:

> …the quick, vigorous measures now adopted and carried out with a firm hand had a magical effect in toning up where there had been demoralization and inspiring confidence where there had been mistrust.[53]

Hooker was proud of the changes that had taken place. He told others that he had "the finest Army on the planet."[54]

Depression and sadness, common after the Battle of Fredericksburg and the Mud March, soon vanished. This picture entitled "a muss" shows soldiers clowning around at the headquarters of the Army of the Potomac.

Lincoln's 4th Visit

APRIL 5–10, 1863

Lincoln kept in constant contact with Hooker throughout the winter and was no doubt pleased with the status of the Army of the Potomac. Surprisingly, according to newspaper reporter Noah Brooks, Lincoln's wife, Mary Todd Lincoln, suggested that he go south and visit the troops in Stafford to boost their morale. Apparently Lincoln took his wife's suggestion, for on April 3rd he wrote to Hooker and said that he would be arriving at his headquarters on Sunday and stay until Tuesday morning. (In actuality, they stayed until Friday.) "Our party will probably not exceed six persons of all sorts."[55]

The party consisted of seven, but they certainly were *of all sorts*, for it included the president, his wife, son Tad, Dr. Anson G. Henry, Captain Crawford, Attorney General Bates and Noah Brooks. All were noteworthy:

Mary Todd Lincoln was not well understood by both sides of the Civil War. Many Union soldiers considered her a traitor as she was a southerner, born in Kentucky. Her stepmother and half-sisters sided with the Confederacy and three of her half-brothers eventually died fighting for the South. Many in the Confederacy did not like her either, as she was married to Lincoln. She endured many criticisms.

Tad Lincoln

Tad Lincoln, named Thomas after Lincoln's father, was soon given the nickname Tad, short for Tadpole. (At birth his head was large and oddly shaped resembling that of a tadpole.) He was known for his mischief and pranks around the White House. It was Tad's 10th birthday, April 4th, when the party departed for Stafford. Historians have not discovered whether the family celebrated at the White House before departure.

Dr. Henry, Lincoln's physician and friend

Dr. Anson G. Henry was Lincoln's medical doctor in Springfield, Illinois, in the 1830s. In 1852, he moved to Oregon, but the two regularly corresponded. While there, Henry split his time between medicine and politics. After becoming president, Lincoln chose his friend to be surveyor-general of Oregon. In 1863, Henry visited the White House on business. Lincoln suggested he accompany him down on his visit of the Army of the Potomac.

Captain Medorem Crawford, also from Oregon, had moved there from New York at age twenty-three. At first he taught Indian children, but later dabbled in farming, business, and politics. In 1861, Lincoln made him Captain and appointed him assistant quartermaster. He became leader of the Emigrant Escort Service which protected wagon trains as they traveled along the Oregon Trail.

Attorney General Edward Bates was born in Virginia, studied in Maryland, and served in the War of 1812. He practiced law in St. Louis and was a one term member of the U.S. House of Representatives. Later he was a Missouri state senator. Lincoln appointed Bates as his attorney general in 1861.

Attorney General
Edward Bates

Noah Brooks was a journalist who originally met Lincoln in 1856 in Dixon, Illinois while covering a political campaign. Later Brooks moved to California. After the death of his wife, in 1862, he was chosen as war correspondent in Washington, D.C. for the *Sacramento Daily Union*. When Lincoln heard that Brooks was in town, he invited him to the White House. The president, after greeting Brooks, said, "Do you suppose I ever forget an old acquaintance? I reckon not."[60] Lincoln made Brooks part of his inner circle, and he became one of his most beloved friends.

Noah Brooks,
Civil War journalist

On Saturday, April 4, 1863, at 5:00 p.m., this unique party boarded the small steamer *Carrie Martin* at the Navy Yard. (Not much is known of the steamer, but during the Civil War many private ships were used for military purposes.) Halfway down the Potomac, it began to snow at such an alarming rate that the crew could not navigate and were forced to anchor for the night in a little cove opposite Indian Head, Maryland, on Prince William County, Virginia's shoreline.

Noah Brooks said that he could not help thinking that the Confederate troops could have easily captured the president that evening, or the entire party for that matter, for there were no guards or precautions taken against such a surprise. After the majority of the party retired, Brooks, Dr. Henry, and Lincoln stayed up until after midnight, "telling stories and discussing matters, political or military in the most free and easy way."[61]

Mary Lincoln also knew much sorrow, for she lost her second son, Edward to tuberculosis in 1850 when he was almost four years old. In 1862, she lost her third son, Willie, to typhoid fever. Afterwards, Mary said criticism could not hurt her since she already endured so much pain.

Despite controversies which swirled around her, Mary regularly visited hospitals. This was extremely dangerous because many of the men were suffering from tuberculosis, typhoid fever, and other contagious diseases.[56] Mary brought the men flowers that were from the White House garden and food prepared in the White House kitchen. While at the hospitals she would read to the wounded and write letters for them.[57]

Mary Lincoln's care for others was also demonstrated by a kindness she showed her private seamstress, Elizabeth Keckley. Elizabeth, a freed slave, became one of Mary's best friends and a confidant. Mary, who was against slavery, gave her seamstress $200 for an association which aided escaped slaves.[58] A letter she wrote her husband discussed her donation:

> I have given her the privilege of investing $200 …in bed covering.
> She is the most deeply grateful being, I ever saw & this sum, I am
> sure, you will not object to being used in the way—The cause of
> humanity requires it.[59]

ARRIVING IN STAFFORD

Sunday, April 5, 1863

By daybreak, the snow had ceased, but it was still chilly and miserable despite it being Easter Sunday. The *Carrie Martin* traveled south and reached Aquia Landing early in the morning. The landing had changed considerably from Lincoln's visit the previous year. The waterfront was now lined with transports and steamers which continually unloaded supplies for over 135,000 troops. Huge warehouses were constructed on the wharf. Daily, one million pounds of forage were unloaded for the over 60,000 horses and mules that were also living in Stafford.

The presidential party was greeted at the wharf by a cheering crowd of saluting soldiers and their family members. The dignitaries entered a crude freight car and sat on rough plank benches. The car, decorated with flags and bunting, was attached to a special waiting train. At 10:00 a.m. they chugged ahead, being cheered again by the enthusiastic crowd.

Lincoln's party passed by Stoneman's Station, also known as Stoneman's Switch.

Traveling along the railroad tracks (the northernmost section of the current Brooke Road) the party noticed that the hills were covered with snow; however, the area was very unwelcoming, as the grounds were cleared of trees. In the distance they could see the endless camps of the soldiers, mostly log structures covered with canvas tents. Although the train did not stop, it passed two railroad stations, Brooke Station (near today's intersection of Rts. 698 and 629) and Stoneman's Switch (east of the junction of Morton and Leeland Roads). At Falmouth Station, the site of Lincoln's first Falmouth visit, the party disembarked. The station was much busier than in April, 1862. It was now a vital station receiving and distributing supplies for the large Army of the Potomac.

Waiting at the station was General Hooker's chief of staff, Major General Daniel Butterfield with two ambulances. Sitting on horseback, as an escort, were Rush's 6th Pennsylvania Lancers. These cavalrymen carried nine-foot long wooden poles tipped with 11-inch steel blades. Scarlet pennants, which topped the eight pound lances, waved in the breeze. Lancers accompanied the president and his party throughout their stay in Stafford.

While riding in a carriage, Lincoln passed the remains of the Phillips House which had burned a month before, the former headquarters of Burnside.

Once boarded, the ambulances traveled east (over today's White Oak Road, Route 218). The well-traveled road was extremely muddy due to the melting snow, so red clay splattered along the way. On Lincoln's left, on a slight hill, he could see the remains of the Phillips House which had been Burnside's headquarters during the Battle of Fredericksburg. The house had accidentally burned. Noah Brooks wrote that the "ruins of that elegant mansion, built in the olden time, added to the sorrowful appearance of the region desolated by war."[62] Continuing along the road the president could also see Little Whim. (A plaque outside the home states that it was Burnside's headquarters, but verification has yet to be found. Later, however, it was headquarters for Provost Marshal General Marsena Patrick.)

Lincoln also rode by Little Whim which still stands today.

About noon, the ambulances pulled up to Hooker's headquarters consisting of rows of tents (northwest of the intersection of Route 218 and Ringgold Road, actually Jenny Lynn and Myers Road). Like most Union commanders, Hooker resisted having quarters better than his men, so he lived in a wall tent or hospital tent, shaped much like a house. On either side of Hooker's tent, similar tents were raised for the presidential party. Noah Brooks said these tents were, "provided with the luxury of a rough board floor, stoves, camp made bedsteads, and real sheets."[63] There were no flags or insignia outside the tents to distinguish the Washington, D.C. celebrities.

Headquarters also included shelters for a topographer, stenographer, and artist. Artists were very important in capturing everyday life as well as immortalizing important battles and ceremonies. People at home were eager to see what their loved ones were doing in the field. Two of the most noted artists depicting the life of the Army of the Potomac were Alfred Waud and Edwin Forbes.

Besides the quarters for the individual men, there were assorted mechanical shops, a telegraph office, bakery, and printing office. The printing office, where orders were printed, was also a wall tent, but large enough for presses and nine employees.

Lincoln's party stayed in tents alongside that of General Hooker.

After settling into his tent, the president decided to stay in camp rather than go exploring the territory, as the weather was still so unpleasant. He did receive the officers of Hooker's staff, shaking each one's hand and exchanging pleasantries. The Lincolns enjoyed themselves at headquarters finding it a nice contrast to the White House. Before evening had ended, young Tad visited practically every tent.

CAVALRY REVIEW

Monday, April 6, 1863

Although the morning was cold and brisk, the President set out on horseback to visit wounded soldiers in the nearest hospital tents, leaving behind kind words and compassion. He would do so for the next two days. By 10 a.m. he received officers of the Army of the Potomac in his tent, just as he had done the night before. By noon he was out on an "elevated plain near Falmouth," for a grand review of the cavalry under the direction of General Stoneman.

Newspapers wrote that the review was on *an elevated plain*, but the exact location is still unknown. There are three possible places where the plain was located. Some soldiers wrote that it was held at General Birney's headquarters.

Birney's headquarters, on April 6th, was in Belle Plain, but he just moved there four days before. His old headquarters was at Bell Air, the site of the recent grand horse race. According to a 1930s WPA report, this possibly could have been the location, for it stated:

> Mrs. Schlemmer [Bell Air owner] has in possession a letter which she values very highly…In the letter she tells about the soldiers being camped here and that President Lincoln was here on this date to review the army with several other noted men. She mentioned President Lincoln's name, but none of the others. It is neatly written and has been well kept.

General Patrick gave yet another location. He wrote that the cavalry review was at Thrashleigh Farm (It was pronounced as Patrick wrote, but the correct spelling was Sthreshley. It was where Grafton Village is located today.)[64]

For this cavalry review, wherever it was held, General Hooker loaned Lincoln a saddle that he received as a gift from *Main and Winchester Saddlers* in San Francisco, California. The general rode a beautiful dark chestnut horse he had recently received from a California friend, but he preferred his light gray war-horse that had been with him during his battles.

Hooker claimed that the cavalry review in Stafford was the largest ever seen in the world.

It must have been an impressive sight for the President to see 13,000–17,000 men on horseback stretching for miles, farther than the eye could see. Nearing the parade ground, he received a 21-gun salute. On one side was the handsome Hooker riding in grand military style. On the other side was General Stoneman, with his flowing beard, wearing a very conspicuous sash across his chest. General Butterfield was behind Hooker, followed by numerous staff and officers. The Lancer escorts added color with their red pennants fluttering in the breeze.

Mrs. Lincoln arrived in a carriage pulled by six horses and took a position at the front of the crowd in which there were about six other ladies on horseback. Little Tad was near the cavalcade wearing boots, spurs and a gray cloak that flew in the gusty wind as he clung onto the saddle of a small pony.

LITTLE "TAD" LINCOLN.

Tad accompanied his father's cavalcade on a small pony.

An American flag was waving in the center of a square where the review would take place. From there the president and the large entourage rode up and down the lines of horses and men taking an hour or two. Whenever the president passed by, colors (regimental flags) were lowered, trumpets blared, swords were drawn, and drums beat. Melting snow caused mud to fly in every direction. A member of the 4th Pennsylvania Cavalry wrote that his unit went to the expense of sending to Aquia Creek for white linen gloves. Ironically, when the review day arrived, "we are obliged to ride through a deep mud pond or slough just before we come to the reviewing officers…"

Later, the president returned to the reviewing area and the troops passed by him. Noah Brooks vividly described the impressive event:

> It was a grand sight to look upon this immense body of cavalry, with banners waving, music crashing, and horses prancing, as the vast column came winding like a huge serpent over the hills past the reviewing party, and then stretching far away out of sight.[65]

After the cavalry passed in review the batteries of horse artillery trotted by. Strong horses and mules pulled heavy pieces of artillery (guns, cannons, howitzers) proudly passed the reviewing stand.

Letters written home from Stafford spoke of the president's appearance:

> …The President made a better appearance on horseback than I expected to see, but he looks extremely thin and careworn, as if his strength would scarcely carry him to the end of his term. (Member of 8th New York Cavalry)

> …looking sick and worn out, dressed in a plain black suit with the tallest of stove-pipe hats, was the President, seated on a fine horse with rich trimmings. (Member of 2nd Massachusetts)

Hooker said the day's festive review was the "biggest" army of men and horses ever seen in the world, "bigger" even than the famous body of cavalry commanded by Marshal Murat[66] (Murat was a cavalry commander under Napoleon Bonaparte.)

That evening Lincoln and his party were serenaded by an army band. This probably pleased the president, as he loved military music.

An Army band, similar to this one, serenaded the President at night.

V CORPS, HOSPITAL VISITS, AND A KISS

Tuesday, April 7, 1863

The third day of Lincoln's visit was cloudy and cool. The president, General Hooker, several commanders, and a company of lancers started the day by reviewing General George Meade's V Corps. (The V Corps area was bounded in the north by Potomac Creek and stretched from modern-day Forbes Street east toward the present railroad track.) This day Lincoln rode a bay horse. A letter sent to the *Rochester Union and Advertiser,* that appeared in their April 14, 1863 issue, said that the president looked "rather care-worn and anxious" as he rode in "a style peculiar to himself. I should think the stirrups were rather short, for his knees were nearly as high as the pommel of his saddle." Evidently, each regiment formed in front of their camps and presented arms as the president passed by.

One of the comments made by a member of the 120th New York Volunteers was particularly revealing:

> …on the 7th "the boys" were out in force to see the President, as he passed through their camp. His thoughtful, honest, care-worn face, lit up at times with a smile while conversing with those near him, impressed them deeply, and many spoke what they felt, that he was indeed the man for the crisis, and fitly chosen to pilot the ship of state safely through the tempestuous seas.

Lincoln visited men in hospital tents by Stoneman's Station.

Later, the president visited the hospital tents near Stoneman's Switch, also called Stoneman's Station. Prior to the Civil War, Stoneman's Switch was just an informal "flag stop" on the R.F. &P. Railroad without buildings. It received its name in November of 1862 when it was established to supply the nearby camps of Union General George Stoneman's III Corps. About half a year later, it became a complex with two canvas-roofed platforms, two sidings, two sheds, a railroad car converted into an office, bakery, and an assortment of tents. This depot was an important Union supply base during the Fredericksburg Campaign and afterwards.[67]

Prior to the president's visit to injured soldiers, a cheer was ordered by Colonel Schoeffel. Lincoln received a very faint one; but soldiers' eyes followed him as he visited each and every tent.

The hospital tents were typically large, well-ventilated structures which contained six beds each. They were arranged in rows, or streets, apart from the rest of the camp. Noah Brooks wrote that under Hooker, who emphasized sanitary regulations, the percentage of sickness in the Army of the Potomac was the lowest in the Union Army.

The president entered each of these neat tents, sat down, and conversed with every man. Removing his hat, he shook hands, asked questions, and listened to their concerns. Brooks' writings show Lincoln's kindness and compassion:

> It was a touching scene, and one to be long remembered, as the largehearted and nobel President moved softly between beds, his face shining with sympathy and his voice often low with emotion. No wonder that these long lines of weary sufferers, far from home and friends, often shed a tear of sad pleasure as they returned the kind salutation of the President and gazed after him with a new glow upon their faces.[68]

After spending most of a day visiting the wounded, he passed by the same soldiers who had given him a weak cheer earlier in the day. This time he received a thunderous cheer from long lines of soldiers. They now appreciated the president after viewing his compassion and empathy.

Although Lincoln had been cheered in the afternoon, he appeared very melancholy that evening. He and his wife attended a gathering at General Sickles' headquarters, Boscobel. (Today there is a subdivision, Boscobel Farms, named for the home which was located at the end of King Georges Grant.) Officers and their wives attending the gala noticed the sadness that seemed to overshadow him. Officers felt that Lincoln made an effort to be cheerful, but his smile was forced. His continence put a gloom on the festivities. General Daniel Sickles, known for his flamboyance, decided to remedy the situation as he called over Princess

Boscobel was the site of a party for the President.

Salm-Salm (pronounced Psalm Psalm). She was the attractive American wife of a Prussian prince who was in command of the 8th New York. Sickles suggested that a surprise kiss from each of the ladies at the party would cheer away the president's sadness. The princess at first resisted the plan, but later consented.

The President was kissed by Princess Salm-Salm

After persuading the ten or twelve ladies present to kiss him too, the princess walked over to Lincoln who was standing beside the fire. How would she ever be able to reach the tall president? Cleverly she asked him to lean forward so she could whisper something in his ear. Instead of a whisper, she kissed him, much to the joy of the party participants. The other ladies followed suit. Laughter and merriment followed for all, except Mary Lincoln. Later to ease the situation, Lincoln said to Sickles, "I am told, General, that you are an extremely religious man." After Sickles denied the accusation, Lincoln cleverly said, "I believe that you are not only a great Psalmist, but a Salm-Salmist."[69]

This picture was taken two days before Lincoln left Springfield for Washington D.C. in 1861.

By 1863, Lincoln had aged considerably. Soldiers who saw him in Stafford said that he looked "careworn."

GRAND REVIEW OF II, III, V, AND VI CORPS

Wednesday, April 8, 1863

The President awoke to another cloudy, cool day. This would be the day of the largest review of all, with over 60,000 men. It would be held on Sthrashley Farm. Preparations were made for days. A large force cleared and leveled a huge field with axes, picks, and shovels. Brush, bushes, and stumps were removed. Ditches were filled and quagmires drained. There was a perfect view of Fredericksburg from the site since virtually all the trees had been previously chopped down by the Union forces in the creation of shelters, roads, and fires.

The Grand Review on April 8th stretched for miles.

This Grand Review included the II, III, V, and VI Corps. Tall stakes with distinctive corps and division badges were placed in the ground of the vast field. These enabled the troops to quickly take position when they arrived.

All morning long, men in new blue uniforms with brightly polished arms streamed on to the field from various parts of Stafford. A May 2, 1863, *Harper's Weekly* article stated:

> ...as the troops marched out upon the field the divisions wheeled into line as if by instinct, with no confusion, no noise, save the music of the bands, the tramp of the regiments, and the few brief orders of the officers.

Hour by hour the force grew larger, and the colorful national and regimental banners grew more numerous. Cold winds swept over the impatient men. Some horses kicked one other. Just when a few of the men were beginning to fall-out, attempting to stay warm by moving, there was the loud boom of cannons. A twenty-one gun salute announced the president's arrival, and the review began.

An artist captured the sight Lincoln witnessed. The review lasted five and a half hours.

The artillery salute frightened the mules. Despite the fact that quartermasters, wagon masters, and teamsters tried to steady them, the mules stampeded amid the well-ordered lines. A New Jersey quartermaster described the scene:

> How the panic-stricken mules did 'whee-haw' and the army wagons 'rattlet-bank that day over the Stafford plains! It was like another battle of Fredericksburg, on a minor scale.[70]

Apparently, Lincoln and Hooker, both on horseback, enjoyed witnessing the comical event. After the excitement of the mules, the cavalcade marched onto the parade ground. Lincoln wore a long, black citizen's frock coat, a fur muffler, and his usual tall hat. Wearing high top boots with spurs, he was mounted on a large bay. Following Lincoln and Hooker were an array of imposing generals, colonels and other officers. The faithful lancers followed behind, eighty strong this day. Mrs. Lincoln arrived in a carriage pulled by four bays. A *Herald* newspaper article said that she was wearing "a rich black dress with narrow flounces, a black cape with broad trimming of velvet around the border and a plain hat of the same hue composed her costume."[71] Her carriage was also accompanied by a squad of lancers who escorted her to a good viewing position. Tad and a new little acquaintance stayed close to Lincoln.

The previous day Tad had met Gus Schurmann who appeared to be his approximate age and height. He was described as a "smooth faced lad" who had come with troops from New Jersey to participate in the war. The lad actually had gone into battles with the rest of the men until General Kearney noticed him and made him his bugler. General Kearney fell, but the boy became the bugler for General Sickles. The young man was outfitted with a sword-belt and sergeant's stripes. He was a favorite among officers, and it was said that they planned to appoint him to a military school as soon as the war was over. (Evidently, Gus later visited Tad at the White House. While in D.C. they saw a play at the Grover's Theater and ironically met John Wilkes Booth backstage.[72])

Lincoln, Hooker, and dignitaries at the review.

First of all the artillery, described as "in splendid condition," was reviewed. The artillery reserve parade consisted of eighty guns each mounted on a gun carriage and pulled by horses. Each gun also had a limber (auxiliary wheels) and towed a caisson (ammunition carrier). There were iron, black Parrott guns that shot 10- and 20-pound projectiles and shiny, brass Napoleon 12-pound smooth bore gun-howitzers, "a favorite of the crowd."

The infantry followed. Each corps was reviewed separately, one division at a time. Their tattered and bullet riddled flags were symbols of pride from previous battles. The men, in seemingly endless columns, saluted the President. Banners dipped, bands struck up *Hail to the Chief,* and bugles sounded. The President consistently touched his hat in a return salute to the officers, but uncovered his head when the enlisted men passed by. Those men waiting to be reviewed tried to stay warm by dancing jigs. Others just rested upon their rifles. General Marsena Patrick, who had met Lincoln in Fredericksburg the year before, was the general officer of the day. He moved from division to division keeping order and supervising the movements of the men. He was described as sitting erect and was "dignified as a Roman" while keeping the troops organized.

The sun came out periodically, casting light on bayonets and rifles which shimmered in the cool air. Those observing the review from a knoll looked on the plain seeing a never-ending trail of men who passed by the president and traveled back to their temporary Stafford shelters. Some soldiers wrote that Confederates in Fredericksburg were attempting to view the splendid occasion from the riverbank and even tried counting the number of men in attendance. Invariably, their southern enemies admired the uniform appearance and weaponry of their blue-clad opponents.

The forces included picturesque Zouave regiments passing in review with their tasseled fezzes, cutaway jackets, red vests, and baggy pants. The president questioned whether or not they stood out to the enemy when fighting. General Hooker replied that their colorful outfits helped unify them and gave them a spirit of pride. He also remarked that they were invaluable fighting men.

Lincoln commented upon the unique hats and dress of the Zouaves. Pictured here are two Zouaves from New York.

This drawing by Edwin Forbes depicts the Zouave uniforms. Colors are annotated.

Many letters written after this Grand Review, mirror those describing Lincoln in earlier reviews. "Careworn" was a commonly used adjective. Excerpts from several letters create a clear description of the president:

> We were reviewed by President Lincoln last Wednesday. The honorable gentleman looked thin and careworn. No doubt it would be a great relief to him as well as to the country at large if the nation was free from the dire calamity of civil war. Perhaps my imagination added the unusual paleness to his cheek, and the expression of care that his countenance wore, but, certainly, as he passed by where we were standing, and I had a chance to see his face fully, I, for the moment doubted the statement, so often made in newspapers, lately, that our President is enjoying the finest health and the best of spirits.[73]

> He wore a tall stovepipe hat, which he had difficulty in keeping on his head. He was so tall and his legs were so long, that while his feet seemed only a foot from the ground, his hat loomed higher than Hooker's head.[74] The poor man looked very wan and pale, and cut an outrageously awkward figure on horse-back, with his stovepipe hat and his elbows stuck out keeping time to the motion of his horse, while his chin seemed almost buried between the knees of his long bony legs. To make it worse, he rode alongside of General Hooker, our new commander, who is remarkably handsome and rides his horse like a centaur.[75]

> As I passed before the now immortal Lincoln and saluted him, I was so exalted physically, and thrilled to every part of my being, I marched past as though lifted up and needed not the earth to walk upon.[76]

> Abraham looks poorly...thin and in bad health...he is to all outward appear-ances much careworn, and anxiety is fast wearing him out, poor man; I could but pity as I looked at him, and remembered the weight of responsibility resting upon his burdened mind; what an ordeal he has passed through, and what is yet before him! All I can say is, Poor Abe! With faith still good in the honest man.[77]

> Our corps with four others, were reviewed by the President—probably one of the finest and grandest reviews ever seen on this continent...The President looked as if he had had hard work to do, being careworn and haggard in appearance.[78]

One soldier wrote that some of the members of his 31st Regiment, New York State Volunteers did not cheer hardily for the President:

> The President appeared to be gratified by the appearance of the troops, but he must have noticed the entire absence of that clamorous enthusiasm which the appearance of "Little Mac" always elicited from us; the absence of enthusiasm is not sign of any decrease...or respect for the President; but we loved McClellan, and we do still love him, and were he to return to us, we should go crazy with delight...It was generally noticed, by the troops present at the review, how thin and care-worn the President looked, poor fellow! I don't wonder at it; the cares of the office...are enough to waste him to a skeleton. Many were the words of sympathy spoken...as he passed along their lines; and if we did not cheer as we used to, our sympathy was none the less warm for him.[79]

Correspondent Noah Brooks reflected upon the five and a half hour review:

> It was a splendid sight to witness these 60,000 men all in martial array, with colors flying, drums beating, and bayonets gleaming in the struggling sunlight, as they wound over hills and rolling ground, coming from miles away, their arms shining in the distance and their bayonets bristling like a forest on the horizon as they disappeared.[80]

Apparently after the review, Brooks also wrote about the chance encounter of emancipated blacks.

> …we suddenly came upon a disorderly and queer-looking settlement of shanties and little tents scattered over a hillside. As the ambulance drove by the base of the hill, as if by magic the entire population of blacks and yellows swarmed out.[81]

The group yelled, "Hurrah for Massa Linkum!" as the party passed by. Mrs. Lincoln asked her husband how many of the "piccaninnies" were named for him.[82] (In America, in the 1840s and 1860s, piccaninny was used to refer to a little child of Black African ethnic origin.[83]) He replied, "Let's see; this is April, 1863. I should say that all those babies under two years of age, perhaps two thirds have been named for me."[84]

PICKETS, BELLE PLAIN, AND THE I CORPS

Thursday, April 9, 1863

Tad told everyone around Hooker's Headquarters that he wanted to see some "graybacks." Early that morning two men from Hooker's staff took Tad and his father down to the Rappahannock River. (Some accounts say that Tad's friend, Gus Schurmann, also accompanied them.) On the shore were Union pickets. Across the river they could see the town still in ruins from the battle four months earlier. A Confederate flag of Stars and Bars waved in the breeze above the wreckage of Fredericksburg. (Interestingly, Lincoln never referred to the Southern opposition as "enemies," "graybacks," or "Confederates" but always called them "rebels.") On the far shore they spotted two Confederate pickets, one was even wearing a light-blue United States Army overcoat. The pickets yelled across that the "Yanks" had been licked at Fort Sumter. Meanwhile a Confederate officer went down see what the yelling was all about and viewed the visitors on the northern shore through a field glass. Whether or not he recognized Lincoln, he took off his hat, bowed and retreated. However, later a Confederate newspaper correspondent quoted a Confederate staff officer as saying that he saw his "Gorillaship" (Lincoln) riding along the picket line."[85]

Union pickets in Stafford are launching a shingle complete with a paper sail and laden with coffee. It will travel across the Rappahannock where Confederate pickets will exchange the coffee for tobacco and return it to the north.

An interesting relationship existed between the pickets on both sides. They affectionately referred to one another as "butternut" and "bluebelly." Surprisingly, they readily traded morning greetings, coffee, newspapers, tobacco, and jackknives with one another. Lincoln even read some of the Southern newspapers during his stay at Hooker's headquarters.

The President passed over many corduroy roads in Stafford similar to this one. The roads enabled heavy pieces of artillery to more easily travel and kept equipment and wagons from getting stuck in mud.

After returning to camp, the president, accompanied by his wife, General Hooker and Noah Brooks, traveled eight miles to Belle Plain to attend a review of the I Corps. This ride was quite an adventure for the president, for he was sitting in an ambulance being pulled by six mules. Much of the way was over rough corduroy roads which caused the president to be jostled and tossed around. (A corduroy road was built of logs laid side by side transversely.) After the mule driver let expletives fly at the mules, Lincoln gently touched the driver on the shoulder and asked, "Excuse me, my friend, are you an Episcopalian?" The startled man answered, "No, Mr. President; I am a Methodist." "Well," said Lincoln, "I thought you must be an Episcopalian, because you swear just like Governor Seward, who is a churchwarden."[86] After that, the ride was a quiet one without profanity.

While traveling to Belle Plain, Lincoln called Brooks' attention to the stumps of trees. He pointed out what he thought was a "good butt," or a good cut, made by an experienced chopper or a bad cut made by an inexperienced chopper. Lincoln's boyhood experiences apparently remained with him for life.

Soldiers wrote that Lincoln passed by White Oak Church on his way to Belle Plain. Today the church is still standing.

Upon reaching Belle Plain, the president viewed a spectacular sight. Appearing before him on this bright, sunny day was a broad, smooth, and level parade ground encircled by partially wooded hills. On the other side was the Potomac Creek, the wide opening to the shimmering Potomac River. A *New York Times* article of April 13th said that the spot selected for the review "was the most romantic to be found in a State abounding in picturesque and attractive scenery. No better place could have been selected to give effect to a large force of troops."

There were two Belle Plains, one in Stafford and one in King George County. Unfortunately, only photographs of the one in King George County are in existence. The Stafford Belle Plain is the inlet located on the top left of this photo.

The landing at Belle Plain was a busy one with ships of all types coming and going. A New York soldier wrote to his sister about Belle Plain saying, "It was a great treat to us boys, to be where we could see the steam boats and vessels going up and down the river. The most of us have not seen a steam boat or a vessel since we left Fort Albany."

According to letters written from Stafford, the president and General Hooker reviewed the I Corps on horseback. Since the president arrived in an ambulance, presumably a horse was waiting for him. A newspaper article said he probably took an ambulance because he was weary from sitting on a saddle for such a long period the day before. A soldier wrote, "The old fellow (Lincoln) rode with his hat in his hand. He looked as though he had a great deal of trouble on his mind." Another wrote, "Uncle Abe is as homely as his pictures represent him in fact the ugliest man I ever saw…" Another soldier who had seen Lincoln in New York two years before wrote:

We saw him when he passed through rochester, during that eventful period preceding his inauguration, and he certainly seems a score of years older to-day than he did then…When Mr. Lincoln smiles or laughs, an immediate change passes over his whole features, and that gravity and dull anxiety of countenance assumes a marked expression of animation and good humor, and the change is great and very apparent.[87]

Lincoln enjoyed hearing military music, like that which was played by this 61st New York Infantry Drum Corps.

As the president rode by the 17,000–20,000 infantry, they presented arms. Later these men and 10–12 artillery batteries passed by Lincoln in review. Stirring music was provided by three brass bands along with numerous drums and fifes. Noah Brooks wrote that, in the I Corps, drums and trumpets or fifes were "preferred by the men for marching as being firmer and more accurate." In some of these drum corps he counted "eight snare drums and thirty trumpets, and in others there were seventy-five or eighty drums and half that number of fifes or piccolos." Brooks reflected upon the sound and said, "One who has not heard such a band can scarcely imagine the glorious and inspiring effect of the roll and beat of so large a number of drums intermingled with the martial blare of the trumpet and the shriek of the ear-piercing fife."[88]

Mary Todd Lincoln rode in an ambulance for this review along with Secretary of Treasury Chase's daughter. One letter described Mary as a "matronly looking woman" with "smiling features, small eyes and very fair complexion."

The 14th Brooklyn Zouaves were in this review, but unlike the Zouaves of the day before, these men had put away their red baggy pants and wore their issued, sky-blue ones; however, they still wore their cutaway jackets. With white gloves, highly polished guns, and fine marching, they made a "splendid appearance."

One soldier wrote that he thought this review was "more brilliant" than the larger review of the previous day, for the weather was beautiful and the surrounding scenery with glistening water added much to the occasion. Letters home, following the review, indicated that the opinion of McClellan was starting to change. A war correspondent for the *Indianapolis Journal* captured this feeling when he wrote, "The health and morale of the army is most excellent. McClellan stock is at a discount. Hooker is at high premium—as high as gold in Wall street."[89]

That evening back at headquarters, Noah Brooks commented that Lincoln was looking rested and in better health. The president replied, "It is a great relief to get away from Washington and the politicians, but nothing touches the tired spot."[90]

REVIEW OF THE XI AND XII CORPS

Friday, April 10, 1863

This day would be the last of Lincoln's six-day visit with the Army of the Potomac. Two reviews, of the XI and XII Corps, would be held before the president and his party departed for Washington.

The morning was clear and cool. The party packed up and left Hooker's Headquarters to travel north for the first review. President and Mrs. Lincoln rode in a carriage drawn by four horses. General Hooker and his staff escorted them. Tad rode ahead of them all. A III Corps soldier from Maine wrote his sister that his division was chosen to escort the president from headquarters. He mentioned that soldiers gathered on each side of a corduroy road and cheered the party as they passed by in the carriage. Evidently, the party first traveled to Camp Sickles (previously called Camp Curtin) located around Boscobel. As they went through camp they were "most heartily cheered by the men off duty." When the party got to one division they saw an arch of evergreens and hanging under it was the word *Welcome*. The road from Camp Sickles to the Stafford Courthouse was a double-track corduroy. Another soldier wrote that this road, likewise, had troops on each side, "strung...nearly as far as I could see each way." The party "rode through at a walk." Three cheers each were given for the President and Mrs. Lincoln and General Hooker. Tad received a *tiger*. (*Three cheers and a tiger* was a common greeting in the 1800s. It meant cheering three times and then growling.) After viewing Lincoln on the road, a soldier commented, "Old Abe looks like the picture of him on the greenbacks, He isn't so homely as some would like to make him. Mrs. Lincoln is rather handsome."

The Brooke Station area was the site where Lincoln reviewed the Eleventh Corps.

Leaving Camp Sickles, the party traveled to Brooke Station arriving about noon. This would be the site of the review of the XI Corps. Approximately 20,000 soldiers attended the event. By this time, the presidential cavalcade had grown quite long. A sergeant wrote, "The president's bodyguard was nearly a half mile in length, consisting of officers, orderlies and cavalrymen." A New York soldier also remarked about the length of the party. There were "enough bodyguards to cover him over twenty times if attacked." Also in the cortège was Vice President Hamlin. It is not recorded if he was at any of the other reviews. The president rode past the troops with his hat off. The same New York soldier said that the President "looks as if he had all he could attend to. I think by the time his time is up he will be ten years older than when he took seat."

Like the I Corps, the XI Corps preferred drums and trumpets or fifes. As a matter of fact, one division under General Schurz abolished brass bands and just had drum and trumpet bands. It was said that his division of Germans marched better than any of the other troops. War correspondent Noah Brooks commented that bands played an important role in soldiers' morale. "Men who are weary with a hard day's march will prick up enough freshness to march many more hours at the striking up of a band of music, even though it be but a drum and fife."[91]

General Darius Couch, commander of the II Corps, sat on horseback next to Lincoln as the XI Corps was being reviewed. Later he reminisced about the day:

It was a beautiful day, and the review was a stirring sight. Mr. Lincoln, sitting
there with his hat off, head bent, and seemingly meditating, suddenly turned to
me and said, 'General Couch, what do you suppose will become of all these men
when the war is over?' And it struck me as very pleasant that somebody had an
idea that the war would some time end.[92]

The second review of the day, of the XII Corps, was held at between 3:00 and
4:00 o'clock. Some letters said that it was held in a large open field near Stafford
Courthouse at Kane's Landing. (A letter written by a soldier from Maryland
gives the location of Kane's Landing. "It is the head of navigation on Aquia
Creek, about one mile east of Stafford Court House, Va. The wharf is a flat boat
tied to a tree, and the landing is a small carbuncle of clay jutting out into the
creek. Great bluffs rise abruptly from the water, on top of which is the camp
of our regiment."[93] Supplies for troops in that area were distributed at Kane's
Landing. They were towed up the creek in canal boats from Aquia Landing by
stern-wheelers.) However, other soldiers wrote that the review of the XII Corps
was at Stafford Courthouse. Wherever the review was held, it consisted of
approximately 15,000–20,000 men.

Prior to Lincoln's arrival, troops practiced drilling like these 110th Pennsylvania soldiers.

A member of the 125th Regiment of Pennsylvania Volunteers wrote about the
preparations for this review, undoubtedly mirroring all regiments in all the reviews:

This visit and inspection by the President was a great occasion. We all labored
to appear our very best: clean clothes, blackened shoes, bright buttons and
burnished guns, told the story of how we appreciated the visit.

It commenced like the other reviews, by firing a twenty-one gun salute. A soldier of the 149th New York Volunteer Infantry wrote, "…when UNCLE ABE hove into sight. He rode with his hat off and looked real natural." Another New York soldier wrote:

> The president sat his horse awkwardly, and his tall figure seemed even taller by the stove-pipe hat he wore. His appearance was in striking contrast to the fine, soldierly bearing of General Hooker, at his side, who rode a beautiful white horse.

The cavalcade consisted of the usual dignitaries–the president, General Hooker, Tad and assorted officers–but it is recorded that at this review Commodore Nutt was also present. A corporal from Pennsylvania wrote to his mother on April 10th:

> President Lincoln has been reviewing the troops here…He has Commodore Nutt with him (a little dwarf that has been on exhibition in Barnum's museum and is only 30 inches tall.) I did not go up today on account of feeling so bad.[94]

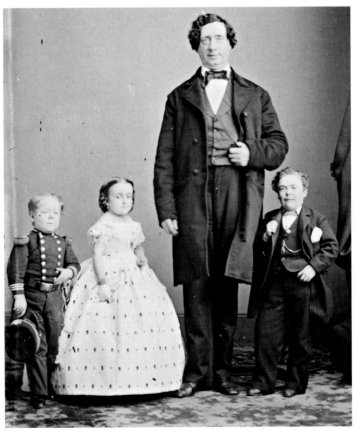

Commodore Nutt, pictured on the left, visited Stafford and helped review troops. Also pictured are Tom Thumb and his wife who were guests at the Lincoln White House after their marriage. The other gentleman, who was probably included for scale, may be Sylvester Bleeker who was P.T. Barnum's agent.

A sergeant from Knap's Pennsylvania Battery witnessed Nutt's presence. He mentioned that:

> The President made his appearance with a large train behind him, Genl. Hooker among the number. He passed in front of all the troops, his son accompanied him, a small boy [possibly Gus Schurmann], and Com. Nutt of Tom Thumb notoriety.[95]

Lincoln was familiar with Commodore Nutt. His real name was George Washington Morrison Nutt. He came to fame when P.T. Barnum hired him in 1862 for the unheard of amount of $30,000 to be a performer at his museum in Florida. Nutt was the best man for Tom Thumb's wedding which was held exactly two months before, on February 10th in New York. The wedding was splashed across newspapers throughout America. Three days after their marriage, Mary Lincoln arranged for Tom Thumb and his wife to visit the White House. It is said that the tall, six-foot-four president bent down kindly to speak to his three-foot four-inch guest. Commodore Nutt may have been one of America's first celebrities to visit troops in the field.

After Lincoln and his party rode through the troops, the troops then passed by in review. A solider wrote:

> It was a grand sight. The men done splendid marching and looked well. Old Abe would bow & take off his hat to each stand of colors, as they passed, several of which looked the worse for wear, and many had a bullet hole through them. Mrs. Lincoln was present in a carriage, in quite a conspicuous place. The President looked care worn & weary, but seemed to be pleased with the appearance of the 12th Corps.[96]

Another soldier wrote about Lincoln's countenance:

> With dressed lines we passed in review under his eye. We cheered lustily under his kindly look and cheerful greeting: we all loved Mr. Lincoln, and a look in his face convinced us of his honesty, and we knew he was an earnest man, a lover of his county, and he was, in addition to all of this, our friend.[97]

There was music at this review too, and Lincoln praised the martial music of both corps this day. Brooks said that the music of the day gave a "most stirring and thrilling effect."[98]

At the conclusion of this second review, Lincoln visited General Oliver O. Howard's XI Corps headquarters at Stafford Courthouse. While there, he and his party had "very good entertainment, cold meats, etc." Lincoln convinced General Sickles and General Schurz to accompany him back to Washington D. C. Evidently, Sickles was riding in a carriage with Mary Lincoln who was extremely quiet, still upset about the kissing incident at Boscobel three nights earlier. Sickles returned to Mary's good graces by telling her stories. Known to be an excellent story teller, he enthralled her by talking about some of his close European friends such as King Louis Philippe, Victor Hugo, and Louis Napoleon.[99]

During this trip, the presidential party rode over the new Potomac Creek Bridge. This sturdier bridge replaced the hastily constructed *Beanpoles and Cornstalks* bridge.

Later, the presidential party boarded a train at Brooke Station for Aquia Landing. When the group reached the landing every steamboat blew its whistle. The party boarded the *Carrie Martin,* the very same steamer that brought them down on April 4th. The ship returned to Washington, D.C. arriving about midnight.

A soldier effectively summarized Lincoln's six day visit by writing, "I doubt if any week in the history of our county has ever witnessed such a large display of fine troops. The army never looked better."[100] A soldier from Massachusetts wrote, "...the Army of the Potomac [is] a collection of as fine troops, I firmly believe, as there are in the world. I believe the day will come when it will be a proud thing for any one to say he belonged to it."

IN WASHINGTON, D.C.

April 11, 1863

The next day, at the White House, it was "business as usual" for the president. In the morning he met with his cabinet and General Halleck to discuss the general military situation. Later he had dinner with the group which returned with him from Stafford. That evening he attended a performance of *Pocahontas* at the Washington Theatre. It was reported in the *Washington Star* April 13, 1863 issue that Lincoln had noticeably laughed. It is unlikely, but not impossible, that the president realized that, when he was at Belle Plain, two days earlier, he was near the actual Pocahontas kidnapping site.

Lincoln's Fifth Visit

RETURNING TO STAFFORD'S SHORE

April 19, 1863

Nine days after Lincoln left Stafford, he returned on a private mission. Departing at pre-dawn from Washington, D.C., with Secretary of War Stanton, he returned the same night. Noah Brooks said the two of them went off on a reconnaissance mission. He thought it was probably to Aquia Creek. Lincoln and Stanton apparently met General Hooker to plan the next move of the Army of the Potomac. In Stafford, General Marsena Patrick wrote in his diary, "…it is announced that the President comes down here this morning to confer with Genl. Hooker—I very much fear the result if Suffolk has fallen…I hope the President may bring us better news…"[101] Brooks also wrote, "What they did, said and saw are matters which agitate the minds of the few who know of the sudden visit. Perhaps it means a change of plan. The day is dark and rainy. Plans are held in abeyance, and the army cannot move…"[102] John G. Nicolay, Lincoln's private secretary also wrote about the secret trip to his assistant, John Hay. "What they did or saw has not transpired."[103]

The troops felt they were ready to fight, as one Pennsylvania soldier wrote:

> It can be truthfully said that a finer army, in better spirits, and more thoroughly disciplined, of over one hundred thousand men, anxious to meet its foe, was never mustered than was the Army of the Potomac in April, 1863, and it impatiently awaited the order to move southward.[104]

In Washington, it was expected that the Army of the Potomac would move out and attack the Confederates, but uncertain weather delayed any action. Noah Brooks wrote:

> From the President down to the newsboys, all watch the signs in the sky with as much anxiety as that which possesses a Wall Street broker during the rise and fall of the gold barometer. Last night with a cloudless and moonlit sky, the President prophesied rain, and the fall flood of today proclaimed Abraham a veritable prophet.[105]

BATTLE OF CHANCELLORSVILLE

On April 29th , Hooker took 73,000 of his men across the Rappahannock into Spotsylvania County to envelope Lee's left flank. Prior to his leaving, he cut the telegraph wires at Aquia Creek and mail was temporarily suspended. Relatives of soldiers, newspaper men, and even the president did not know what was going on. (Given the discussions between Hooker and Lincoln on the 19th, it is likely that Lincoln was at least generally aware of Hooker's plans and intentions but may have lacked the details.) As Brooks wrote, "We are still hungering and thirsting after news from the Army of the Potomac and find but a precious little of it. Nobody knows anything 'for certain,' not even the Secretary of War himself..."[106]

The White House was buzzing with conjecture about what was happening at Chancellorsville. (Earliest known view of White House, photographed in the 1860s)

By May 3rd, two days into the battle, General Butterfield, Hooker's chief of staff, telegraphed Lincoln in the morning that "a battle is in progress." That afternoon he reported, "General Hooker is at Chancellorsville."

It was three o'clock in the afternoon on Wednesday, May 6th, three days later, when the War Department received the next dispatch from General Butterfield. The army had lost at Chancellorsville, withdrawn from the Spotsylvania side of the Rappahannock, and returned to their Stafford camps.[107]

Brooks was at the White House in a room sitting with Lincoln's dear friend Dr. Henry when the president opened the door a little after three. He held a message in his hand. According to Brooks, Lincoln's face was ashen. As a matter of fact, he blended into the "French gray" wallpaper behind him. Closing the door, he had Brooks read aloud the dispatch from Butterfield. Later, Brooks wrote that as he read the words the president's appearance was "piteous."

> Never, as long as I knew him, did he seem to be so broken, so dispirited,and so ghostlike. Clasping his hands behind his back, he walked up and down the room, saying, "My God! My God! What will the country say! What will the country say!"[108]

The president hurriedly left the room. Dr. Henry, upon seeing his friend's reaction to the news, started crying. While Brooks tried to console him, he noticed a carriage coming up to the White House and could see Lincoln darting into the vehicle. Shortly thereafter, an attendant told them that the president and General Halleck were leaving immediately for the Army of the Potomac.

Lincoln's Sixth Visit

THE PRESIDENT'S FINAL TRIP TO STAFFORD

May 7, 1863

Lincoln and Halleck arrived at the Navy Yard in pouring rain. At four o'clock the two took a special steamer for their trip south.

In D.C., news of the army's failure had spread by nightfall. Rumors flew about. "Lincoln went down to put Hooker under arrest." "Stanton had resigned." "Lee injured Hooker and was approaching D.C." Brooks wrote that the "McClellanites and secessionists (they are about the same thing) who had prophesied defeat and disaster sprang to new life and animation and with smiling faces and ill-suppressed joy were dotted through the gloomily excited crowds."[109]

Exactly what went on at Aquia Landing was unknown. It is thought that Lincoln and Halleck got off the ship and visited immediately with troops. For when Lincoln returned at night from his visit, according to Noah Brooks, "he thinks the troops are none the worse for the campaign."[110] He did contact Hooker on that date. A portion of Lincoln's message said:

> The recent movement of your army is ended without effecting its object …What next? …Have you already in your mind a plan wholly, or partially formed? If you have, prosecute it without interference from me. If you have not, please inform me, so that I, incompetent as I may be, can try [to] assist in the formation of some plan for the Army. Yours as ever A LINCOLN."[111]

A copy of Hooker's reply is preserved in the Lincoln Papers in an envelope endorsed by Lincoln, "Gen. Hooker. Visit to camp, May 7 1863." Part of Hooker's reply is as follows:

> As to the best time for renewing our advance upon the enemy, I can only decide after an opportunity has been afforded to learn the feeling of the troops. They should not be discouraged or depressed, for it is not fault of theirs—if I may except one Corps—that our last efforts were not crowned with glorious victory. I suppose details are not wanted of me at this time.[112]

General Marsena Patrick wrote in his journal about Lincoln's May 7th visit:

> The President & Gen. Halleck have been here today and I understand that the whole thing has been represented by Hooker as a grand Success and Abraham has gone back well pleased with every thing.[113]

Soldiers requested Lincoln give them a 100 pound cannon.
Shown here, on Stafford Heights, are thirty-two pounders.

The I Corps artillery chief also wrote in his journal about the presidential visit:

> I hear that Mr. Lincoln has been down here, and that finding the "Seven Sisters" [small artillery] could not reach a fifty-pounder [cannon] the enemy have on the heights opposite, he declared he would send down a hundred-pounder on his own responsibility. I should think that, if we have to move in a hurry, Hooker might find it very much like a present of an elephant.[114]

Evidently, Lincoln remembered the promise he made to the troops that May evening in Stafford. Later in June, Elisha Hunt Rhodes wrote:

> On a hill on the north side of the Rappahannock River our people had mounted a 100 lb. rifle gun. It took several days to get the gun in position. Just before dark its only shot was fired. The recoil upset the gun, and as the Army was to move, the gun was sent to the rear. This shot passed over the river, over our heads, and into a Rebel fort on the hill near Fredericksburg. It burst and sent up a cloud of sand and dust. The noise it made was like that of a railroad train, and when it struck the whole army cheered.[115] (On display at the White Oak Civil War Museum is a partial 100 lb. ball that was found near the Shannon Airport in Fredericksburg. This might be the one fired that night.)

IN WASHINGTON, D.C.

Chancellorsville Facts Come In

Meanwhile statistics were coming in concerning the Chancellorsville Campaign. The Union forces numbered 97,382 men. (It is interesting to note that this number is considerably less than that given to Lincoln when he was in Stafford. On April 6th Hooker claimed to have 136,724 men present for duty.[116]) The Confederate force of 57,352 was a good deal less. The number of those who perished was surprisingly equal; 1,575 Union troops and 1,665 Confederates troops. The Union had 9,594 wounded while the Confederates had an almost equal amount of 9,081. However, the number of missing was very lopsided: Union 5,676 and Confederates 2,018. General Darius Couch later reminisced what Lincoln had said previously:

> Before he [Lincoln] went away he sent for Hooker and for me, I being second in command, and almost his last injunction was, 'Gentlemen, in your next battle *put in all your men.*' Yet that is exactly what we did not do at Chancellorsville.[117]

Perhaps Chancellorsville would have had a better outcome had Hooker heeded Lincoln's advice.

Regardless of how troubled the president was with the war, he always took time to display kindness. For example, he discovered that a young soldier from Massachusetts had his life saved at Chancellorsville by his pocket Bible. A rifle ball became imbedded in the Bible which lay over the soldier's heart. Therefore, the president sent the lad another Bible and inscribed it. Perhaps he inscribed it like he did for a young girl from Ohio. Annie Harries had asked for the president's autograph. Not having paper handy she handed him a pocket Bible she had in her purse. He signed, "Live by the words within these covers—and you will be forever happy. Yours truly, A. Lincoln."[118]

Lincoln's Stafford Visits Make History

As far as we know, President Lincoln never returned to Stafford. However, he attempted to return on Saturday, June 13, 1863. At 1 p.m., Lincoln and Quartermaster General Montgomery Meigs, boarded a tug at the Navy Yard for a trip south to view a demonstration of incendiary shells at Hooker's headquarters. Hooker had telegraphed the president the day before stating, "It will give me great pleasure to have the gun on exhibition …I have some good targets in the shape of rebel camps which the gun will enfilade."[119] Presumably, Hooker changed his mind when he discovered General Robert E. Lee was moving into Pennsylvania. He telegraphed the president, "It may be well not to come." Since Lincoln and Meigs were already underway, Stanton telegraphed Captain Ferguson at Alexandria stating, "Stop the tug on which the president is and ask him to return."[120] The tug turned around and reached Washington, D.C. at 3:30 p.m.

The next day Hooker's troops thronged to Aquia Landing and evacuated Stafford. Once equipment, supplies, and men were loaded and headed up north, empty warehouses on the landing were set on fire. The Army of the Potomac had departed Stafford, but the memories of Lincoln's visits remained with the army forever.

Lincoln's visits to Stafford played a critical role in interaction with his generals and played a significant role in encouraging the troops. Author and professor Chandra Miller Manning writes insightfully that Lincoln's visits to the troops displayed his compassion, accessibility, and lack of pretension. She adds:

> …the spectacle of the hapless president filled the soldier with affection for a national leader who placed so little stock in looking superior…The President's personal appearance further endeared Lincoln to soldiers because his haggard looks convinced soldiers that he, too, had suffered, and would sympathize with their plight.[121]

His visits also changed political history, as Lincoln was reelected president in 1864. His Democratic challenger was none other than "Little Mac", General George McClellan. Prior to Lincoln's visits, the army had adored McClellan. Some even left the Army when Lincoln replaced him. Others spoke of mutiny. The change in the Army's feelings toward McClellan probably would never have occurred without Lincoln's mingling with and bolstering the Army of the Potomac. This book only emphasizes the President's main Corps reviews, but it is recorded that he frequently left Hooker's headquarters and rode throughout various camps. The troops saw his compassion and tenderness during his visits.

They appreciated his kind words and gentle smile. Morale had previously been at an all time low after the Battle of Fredericksburg and the disastrous Mud March. Hooker's positive command changes and Lincoln's visits helped reinvigorate the troops. Since there were over 135,000 Union soldiers in Stafford, many thousands of letters were sent home describing Lincoln's compassionate actions while visiting the county. This probably helped influence the attitude of people at home toward the president and, in turn, influenced their subsequent 1864 voting.

Voting was made available for troops in the field. Lincoln defeated McClellan and was reelected.

The facts of the November election were quite impressive. McClellan only received electoral votes from three out of the twenty-five states. A *Harper's Weekly* article dated November, 1864 stated:

> Lincoln's popular majority was 411,428. In the twelve states whose vote by soldiers was counted so as to be distinguished, the success of the administration was even more signal, its majority being over 3 to 1. [Lincoln 119,754– McClellan 34,291] Such was the decision of the soldiers on the questions of peace and emancipation.

War was still raging when the election was held. If McClellan had won, he might possibly have negotiated peace as his Democratic party proposed. He, too, might have returned the South's economy to slavery, as he felt slavery was protected under the law. American history might have changed dramatically if McClellan won. Lincoln's visits permanently impacted our nation. Lincoln fulfilled his role as Commander-in-Chief by conferring with his generals at key junctures. He bolstered the morale of the Army of the Potomac at a critical point in the war and solidified his political base with his soldiers for the November election. Lincoln's Stafford visits were important in defining American history.

MAP OF LINCOLN'S TRAVELS
IN STAFFORD COUNTY

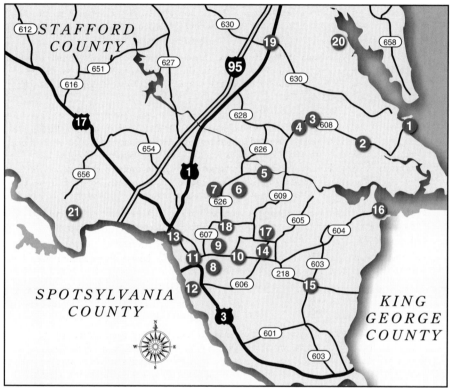

Steven Stanley/Colonial Design and Graphics/Gettysburg, PA

1. **Aquia Landing** (end of Rt. 608) Steamboat landing site in 1815. Became terminus of the RF&P Railroad in 1842. First Civil War Naval skirmish in May of 1861. Place where Lincoln arrived at Stafford and where he departed on each visit.

2. **Brooke Road** (Rt. 608) Northernmost portion is the former RF&P Railroad bed. Lincoln rode over the rails here.

3. **Brooke Station** (Intersection of Rt. 608 and Rt. 629) Supply depot for XI and XII Corps and Headquarters for XI Corps. Lincoln first rode by this station on his way to Falmouth in 1862. He was here for review on April 10, 1863.

4. **Accokeek Bridge** (located where today's Brooke Road crosses over Accokeek Creek). In 1862, bridge was rebuilt by Herman Haupt and troops in an amazing 15 hours.

5. **Potomac Creek Bridge** (Rt. 625) Site of the famous *Beanpoles and Cornstalks Bridge* over which Lincoln walked.

6. **Stoneman's Switch or Station** (Rt. 626 north of present railroad tracks, opposite Rt. 624) Station was a large supply depot serving the III and V Corps. Lincoln visited men in nearby hospital tents.

7. **Bell Air Site** (Nearby Conway Elementary, off Rt. 626) Used as a headquarters by Union generals.

8. **Falmouth Station Site** (1/10 mile south of Rt. 218 on Cool Spring Rd., near today's Fraternal Order of Eagles Lodge) Where Lincoln stopped on several trips to Falmouth. This railroad station served as a Union supply depot for the area.

9. **Phillips House Site** (Northside Drive, 1/10 mile north of Rt. 218) Headquarters for Burnside during Battle of Fredericksburg. Accidentally burned in February of 1863, Lincoln passed by and noticed house. A private home is now on the site.

10. **Little Whim** (Rt. 218, east of Phillips House) Lincoln passed by this lovely house in 1863. Remarkably, one of the few frame houses still standing after war in Stafford. Said to be Burnside's Headquarters too, but for sure was headquarters for General Marsena Patrick. Currently a private home.

11. **Chatham/ Lacy House** (Chatham Lane) This Georgian manor, built in 1771, was known as the Lacy House during the Civil War. On May 23, 1862, Lincoln visited the house. He met commanders inside the house and visited troops encamped around the house. It was the headquarters for both McDowell (April-August 1862) and Burnside (August 1862). Sumner's right grand division was headquartered there in November 1862-January 1863. Only private home in America visited by Washington, Jefferson, and Lincoln. It is owned by the National Park Service and is open daily to the public. Free Admission.

12. **Ferry Farm / George Washington's Boyhood Home** (Rt. 3, east of Chatham Bridge) Site of the farm where George Washington grew up from the age of six to adulthood. Lincoln passed over site in May of 1862. Open to public. Admission fee.

13. **Falmouth** (area around Rt. 1 and U.S. Rt. 17) Many Colonial and Antebellum homes and buildings spared destruction due to Union occupation.

14. **Hooker's Headquarters Site** (northwest of junction Rt. 218 and Rt. 606) General Hooker set up Army of the Potomac Headquarters here on the Curtis farm. This was the site of Lincoln's stay for six day visit.

15. **White Oak Civil War Museum / White Oak Church** (Rt. 218 and Newton Road) This museum contains thousands of Civil War artifacts discovered in Stafford County. Displays of dugout shelters are on the grounds and in the museum. Open to public for minimal admission. White Oak Church (across Rt. 218) was established in 1789. Thousands of tents of VI Corps radiated out from church. Church is privately owned.

16. **Belle Plain Landing - today called Bell Plains** (end of Rt. 604, Belle Plains Road) Lincoln reviewed I Corps here on April 9, 1863. The landing was a major Union supply base and hospital site.

17. **Boscobel Home Site** (was at the end of King Georges Grant) Home was the site of the famous kiss given to Lincoln by Princess Salm-Salm.

18. **Sthreshley** (pronounced Thrashleigh) **Farm Site,** now considered Grafton Village area. Site of Lincoln's Grand Review of II, III, V, and VI Corps.

19. **Stafford Courthouse** (Intersection of Rt. 630 and U.S. 1) The present day courthouse was built in 1922; it sits upon wartime courthouse site. Nearby Lincoln reviewed XII Corps.

20. **Kane's Landing** was a small landing on Aquia Creek, north of Aquia Landing. Some soldiers said that it was here where XII Corps was reviewed.

21. **Mud March Area** Attempting to march east on Warrenton Road (today's U.S. 17) to attack Lee's flank, Burnside's troops turned south at the Greenbank Farm. He wanted them to cross at Bank's Ford, near today's Celebrate Virginia's golf course, Cannon Ridge.

NOTES

1   Homer D. Musselman, *Stafford County in the Civil War* (Fredricksburg: Bookcrafters, HE. Howard, Inc.,1995), 3-4

2   Musselman 2.

3   Musselman 6-10.

4   Paul H. Silverstone, *Warships of the Civil War Navies* (Annapolis: Naval Institute Press, 1989), 188.

5   Robert J. Schneller, *A Quest for Glory: A Biography of Rear Admiral John A. Dahlgren* (Annapolis: Naval Institute Press, 1996), 186.

6   Madeleine V. Dahlgren, *Memoir of John A. Dahlgren* (Boston: James R. Osgood and Co., 1882), 364.

7   Noah Brooks, *Mr. Lincoln's Washington,* ed. P.J. Staudenraus, (New York: Thomas Yoseloff, 1967) 34.

8   Earl Schenck Miers, ed., *Lincoln Day by Day, A Chronology* (Dayton: Morningside, 1991), 107.

9   Herman Haupt, *Reminiscences of General Herman Haupt* (North Stratford, NH: Ayer Co. Publ. Inc, reprint ed., 2000), 43.

10   Haupt 46.

11   Haupt 48.

12   Haupt 47.

13   Haupt 48.

14   Dahlgren 368.

15   Dahlgren 368 fn 1.

16   Dahlgren 369.

17   Haupt 49.

18   Noel G. Harrison, *Fredericksburg Civil War Sites,* Vol. 1 (Lynchburg: H.E. Howard, Inc., 1995), 84.

19   Temperance Address, 22 February 1842, in Roy P. Basler, ed., *The Collected Works of Abraham Lincoln,* vol. 1 (New Brunswick, N.J., 1953-55) 279.

20   William C. Davis, *Lincoln's Men* (New York: The Free Press, 1999) 3.

21   Abraham Lincoln, *The Lincoln Encyclopedia* ed. Archer H. Shaw (New York: The MacMillan Co., 1950) 369.

22   *The Christian Banner,* Fredericksburg, VA, 31 May 1862.

23   Ronald Johnson and Harlan D. Unrau, eds. *Preliminary Historic Resource Study, Chatham* (Denver: NPS, 1982) 124 fn 19.

24   David S. Sparks, ed., *Inside Lincoln's Army: The Diary of Marsena Rudolph Patrick* (New York: Thomas Yoseloff, 1964) 82.

25   John T. Goolrick, *Historic Fredericksburg; The Story of an Old Town* (Richmond: Whittet & Shepperson,1922) 162.

26   Dahlgren 369.

27   Colonel John N. Macomb, May 23, 1862 letter to daughter Minerva, Rodgers Family Papers, Library of Congress.

28   Dalgren 370.

29 Musselman 20.

30 Haupt 146.

31 Don C. Pfanz, *War So Terrible, A Popular History of the Battle of Fredericksburg* (Richmond: Page One Inc. 2003) 14.

32 P. Basler, 511.

33 Official Records, Series I, vol. 21 (Washington, D.C.:Library of Congress) 798.

34 Silverstone 107.

35 Miers 152.

36 Civil War Letters of Corporal Adam Muenzenberger, 1862. http://www.russscott.com/~rscott/26thwis/adamlett.htm

37 Jeffry D. Wert, *The Sword of Lincoln; The Army of the Potomac* (New York: Simon & Schuster, 2005) 210.

38 Russell Freedman, *Lincoln, A Photobiography* (New York: Clarion Books, 1987) 91.

39 Lincoln 108.

40 Henry County, Indiana Genealogy and History Web site: http://www.rootsweb.com/~inhenry/ letters 1863.

41 Bruce Catton, *Picture History of the Civil War* (New York: American Heritage Pub. Co.,1960) 281.

42 Time Life editors, *Voices of the Civil War; Fredericksburg.* (Alexandria, VA: Time Life Books, 1997) 156.

43 (Capt. Samuel Fiske wrote to the *Springfield Republican* and signed the papers Dunn Brown.) *Mr. Dunn Brown's Experiences in the Army; the Civil War letters of Samuel W. Fiske,* ed. Stephen Sears (New York: Fordham University Press, 1998).

44 Carl Sandburg, *The War Years,* vol. 1 (New York: Harcourt, Brace & World, Inc., 1939) 84.

45 K. Jack Bauer, ed., *Soldiering; The Civil War Diary of Rice C. Bull, 123rd New York Volunteer Infantry* (San Rafael: Presidio Press, 1977) 32.

46 James P. Brady, comp., *Hurrah for the Artillery!: Knap's Independent Battery "E, Pennsylvania Light Artillery* (Gettysburg: Thomas Publications, 1992) letter by James P. Stewart, Feb 10, 1863, 197.

47 St. Clair Mulholland, *A Story of the 116th Regiment Pennsylvania Volunteers in the War of Rebellion* (Philadelphia: McManus, Jr. & Co., 1903) 77.

48 Oliver Wilson Davis, *Life of David Bell Birney, Major-General United States Volunteers* (Philadelphia: King & Baird, 1867) 126.

49 Gilbert Adams Hays, comp., *Under the Red Patch; Story of The Sixty Third Regiment Pennsylvania Volunteers* (Pittsburg: 63rd Penn. Vol. Reg. Assoc., 1908) 176.

50 Davis 127.

51 Davis 119.

52 Thomas Chamberlin, *History of the One Hundred and Fiftieth Regiment; Pennsylvania Volunteers* (Philadelphia: F. McManus, Jr. & Co., 1905) 176.

53 *Battles and Leaders of the Civil War,* vol. 3, (New York: Thomas Yoseloff, Inc., 1956), 154.

54 Sandburg 84.

55 Basler, vol 6, 161.

56 John Lockwood, "History, Soldiers see First Lady Differently" *The Washington Times,* 1 July, 2006.

57   Dan Santow, *Mary Todd Lincoln* (New York: Children's Press, 1999) 70.

58   Santow 70.

59   David Herbert Donald, *Lincoln at Home* (Washington, D.C.: Thornwillow Press, 1999) 68.

60   Noah Brooks, *Washington in Lincoln's Time* (New York: Rinehart & Co., Inc., 1958) 10.

61   Brooks 51.

62   Brooks 58.

63   Noah Brooks, *Mr. Lincoln's Washington*, P.J. Staudenraus, ed. (New York: Thomas Yoseloff, 1967) 150.

64   Sparks 231.

65   Brooks, *Wash. In Lincoln's Time,* 53

66   Brooks 53.

67   Noel G. Harrison, *Gazetteer of Historic Sites,* manuscript collections, FRSP, volume 180, pg. 146-147.

68   Brooks, *Mr. Lincoln's Washington*, 158.

69   Don E. and Virginia Fehrenbacher, *Recollected Words of Abraham Lincoln* (Stanford, CA: Stanford University Press, 1996) *New York Tribune*, 21 May 1899, 406.

70   James F. Rusling, *Men and Things I Saw in the Civil War Days* (New York: Eaton & Mains Press, 1899) 11.

71   Sanburg 90.

72   Ralph Gary, *Following in Lincoln's Footsteps* (New York: Carroll & Graf Pub., 2001) 355.

73   Emil and Ruth Rosenblatt, eds., *Hard Marching Every Day* (Laurence, KA: University Press of Kansas, 1983) 64.

74   Bauer 33.

75   Thomas Francis Galwey, *The Valiant Hours.* ed. W.S. Nye (Harrisonburg: The Stackpole Company, 1961) 82.

76   George W. Sherman, *A Narrative of War Time, 20th Connecticut Volunteer Infantry* (Lynbrook, NY: New Era Press, 1917) 31.

77   Carter, Robert, *Four Brothers in Blue* (Austin: University of Texas Press, 1978) 237.

78   Letter of R.E. to *Rochester Democrat and American,* 18 April 1863, printed 28 April 1863..

79   William B. Styple, ed., *Writing and Fighting the Civil War* (Kearney, NJ: Belle Grove Pub. Co., 2000) 183

80   Brooks 158-159.

81   Brooks, *Washington in Lincoln's Time* 59.

82   Brooks 60.

83   J.A. Simpson and E.S.C. Weiner preps., *The Oxford English Dictionary.* Sec. Edition, vol. 6, (Oxford: Clarendon Press, 1989) 763.

84   Brooks 60.

85   Gary 314.

86   Brooks 55.

87   10 April 1863 letter of Lt. George Breck published in *Rochester Union and Advertiser.* John Hennessy and Richard Becker, compiled and transcribed.

88   Brooks, *Mr. Lincoln's Washington*, 162.

89   *Richmond* (Indiana) *Palladium*, 24 April 1863, 2.

90   Brooks, *Washington in Lincoln's Time*, 55.

91   Brooks, *Mr. Lincoln's Washington*, 162.

92   Darius N. Couch, "The Battle of Fredericksburg," *The Century War Book* (New York: Arno Press, 1978) 169.

93   *American and Commercial Advertiser,* Vol. CXXVII, No. 20,779, 11April 1863, 4.

94   Brady 208.

95   Brady 209.

96   Brady 209.

97   Regimental Committee, comp., *History of the One Hundred and Twenty-fifth Regiment Pennsylvania Volunteers 1862-1863* (Philadelphia: J.B. Lippincott Co., 1906) Letter by JD Hicks, 127.

98   Brooks, *Washington in Lincoln's Time*, 56.

99   Thomas Keneally, *American Scoundrel; The Life of the Notorious Civil War General Dan Sickles* (New York: Doubleday, 2002) 225.

100 Milo M. Quaife, *From the Cannon's Mouth: The Civil War Letters of Alpheus S. Williams* (Lincoln: University of Nebraska Press, 1995) Letter of 14 April 1863.

101 Sparks 234-235.

102 Brooks, *Mr. Lincoln's Washington*, 167.

103 John G. Nicolay Papers, 20 April 1863, Library of Congress, Washington, D.C.

104 Regimental Comm., 126

105 Brooks 172.

106 Brooks 173-174.

107 Basler vol. 6, 3 May1863.

108 Brooks, *Washington in Lincoln's Time*, 61.

109 Brooks, *Mr. Lincoln's Washington*, 180.

110 Miers 7 May 1863.

111 Basler vol. 6, 201.

112 Basler vol. 6, 201.

113 Sparks 244.

114 Allan Nevins, ed., *A Diary of Battle; The Personal Journals of Colonel Charles S. Wainwright, 1861-1865.* (Gettysburg: Stan Clark Military Books, 1962) 217.

115 Robert Hunt Rhodes, ed., *All for the Union; The Civil War Diary and Letters of Elisha Hunt Rhodes* (New York: Orion Books, 1991) 113.

116 William C. Davis, *Lincoln's Men; How President Lincoln Became Father to an Army and a Nation* (New York: The Free Press, 1999) 140.

117 Couch 169.

118 *Lincoln Herald, Commemorative Issue 1897-1997,* Spring, 1997. (Harrogate, TN: Lincoln Memorial University Press).

119 Official Reports, OR, I,XXVII, 1, 37.

120 Collected Works of Abraham Lincoln, Vol. 6, June 13, 1863

121 Chandra Miller Manning, "Like a Handle on a Jug" *North and South Magazine.* vol. 9, no. 4, 36.

BIBLIOGRAPHY

Basler, Roy P., Marion Dolores Pratt, and Lloyd A. Dunlap, eds. *The Collected Works of Abraham Lincoln*. 9 vols. New Brunswick, NJ: Rutgers University Press, 1953.

Bauer, K. Jack, ed. *Soldiering; The Civil War Diary of Rice C. Bull, 123rd New York Volunteer Infantry*. San Rafael: Presidio Press, 1977.

Boyce, C.W. *A Brief History of the Twenty-eight Regiment New York State Volunteers*. Buffalo: Matthews-Northrup Co., 1896.

Brady, James P., comp. *Hurrah for the Artillery!; Knap's Independent Battery E, Pennsylvania Light Artillery*. Gettysburg: Thomas Publications, 1992.

Brooks, Noah. *Washington in Lincoln's Time*. New York: Rinehart & Company, Inc., 1958.

___. *Mr. Lincoln's Washington*. Ed. P.J. Staudenraus, New York: Thomas Yoseloff, 1967.

Carter, Robert. *Four Brothers in Blue*. Austin: University of Texas Press, 1978.

Catton, Bruce. *Picture History of the Civil War*. New York: American Heritage Publishing Co., 1960.

Chamberlin, Thomas. *History of the One Hundred and Fiftieth Regiment; Pennsylvania Volunteers*. Philadelphia: F. McManus, Jr. & Co., 1905.

Couch, Darius N. "The Battle of Fredericksburg," *The Century War Book*. New York: Arno Press, 1978.

Dahlgren, Madeleine V. *Memoir of John A. Dahlgren*. Boston: James R. Osgood and Company, 1882.

Davis, Oliver Wilson. *Life of David Bell Birney, Major-General United States Volunteers*. Philadelphia: King & Baird, 1867.

Davis, William C. *Lincoln's Men; How President Lincoln Became Father to an Army and a Nation*. New York: The Free Press, 1999.

Donald, David Herbert. *Lincoln at Home*. Washington, D.C.: White House Historical Association with cooperation of Thornwillow Press, 1999.

Fehrenbacher, Don E. and Virginia. *Recollected Words of Abraham Lincoln*. Stanford, CA: Stanford University Press, 1996.

Freedman, Russell. *Lincoln, A Photobiography*. New York: Clarion Books, 1987.

Galwey, Thomas Francis. *The Valiant Hour*. Ed. W.S. Nye. Harrisburg: The Stackpole Company, 1961.

Gary, Ralph. *Following in Lincoln's Footsteps*. New York: Carroll & Graf Publishers, 2001.

Getz, Elizabeth. "'Take a Good Ready and Start Monday Mornings'; Abraham Lincoln in Fredericksburg, May 1862". *The Journal of Fredericksburg History*. vol. 9. Fredericksburg: Historic Fredericksburg Foundation, 1999.

Goolrick, John T. *Historic Fredericksburg: The Story of an Old Town*. Richmond: Whittet & Shepperson, 1922.

Griffin, William E., Jr. *Along the Richmond, Fredericksburg and Potomac Railroad*. Richmond: Whittet & Shepperson, 1984.

Harrison, Noel G. *Gazeteer of Historic Sites*. Vol.180. Fredericksburg and Spotsylvania National Military Park Manuscript Collection. 1986.

___. *Fredericksburg Civil War Site*. 2 vols. Lynchburg, VA: H.E. Howard, Inc., 1995.

Haupt, Herman. *Reminiscences of General Herman Haupt.* North Stratford, NH: Ayer Company Publishers, Inc., reprint ed. (1901) 2000.

Hays, Gilbert Adams, comp. *Under the Red Patch; Story of The Sixty Third Regiment, Pennsylvania Volunteers.* Pittsburg: 63rd Penn. Vol. Reg. Assoc., 1908.

Johnson, Ronald, and Harlan D. Unrau, eds. *Preliminary Historic Resource Study, Chatham.* Denver: NPS, U.S. Dept. of the Interior, 1982.

Keneally, Thomas. *Abraham Lincoln.* New York: A Lipper ™/Viking Book, 2003.

___. *American Scoundrel: The Life of the Notorious Civil War General Dan Sickles.* New York: Doubleday, 2002.

Manning, Chandra Miller. "Like a Handle on a Jug; Union Soldiers and Abraham Lincoln" *North and South Magazine.* Vol. 9, no. 4, August, 2006, 34-46.

Marvel, William. *Burnside.* Chapel Hill: The University of North Carolina Press, 1991.

Miers, Earl Schenck, ed. *Lincoln Day by Day, A Chronology.* Dayton, Ohio: Morningside, 1991.

Mills, Eric. *Chesapeake Bay in the Civil War.* Centreville, Maryland: Tidewater Publishers, 1996.

Mulholland, St. Clair. *A Story of the 116th Regiment Pennsylvania Volunteers in the War of Rebellion. Philadelphia: McManus, Jr & Co., 1903.*

Musselman, Homer D. *Stafford County in the Civil War.* Lynchburg, VA: H.E. Howard, Inc., 1995.

Nevins, Allan, ed. *A Diary of Battle; The Personal Journals of Colonel Charles S. Wainwright, 1861-1865.* Gettysburg: Stan Clark Military Books, 1962.

Newman, Ralph and E.B. Long. *The Civil War.* Vol. 2. New York: Grosset & Dunlap, Inc, 1956.

Pfanz, Donald C. *War So Terrible; A Popular History of the Battle of Fredericksburg.* Richmond: Page One Inc., 2003.

Quaife, Milo M., ed. *From the Cannon's Mouth: The Civil War Letters of Alpheus S. Williams.* Lincoln: University of Nebraska Press, 1995.

Regimental Committee, comps. *History of the One Hundred and Twenty-fifth Regiment Pennsylvania Volunteers 1862-1863.* Philadelphia: J.B. Lippincott Company, 1906.

Rhodes, Robert Hunt, ed., *All for the Union; The Civil War Diary and Letters of Elisha Hunt Rhodes.* New York: Orion Books, 1991.

Rosenblatt, Emil and Ruth, eds. *Hard Marching Every Day.* Laurence, Kansas: University Press of Kansas, 1983.

Sanburg, Carl. *The War Years.* Vol. 2, New York: Harcourt, Brace & World, Inc.,1939.

Santow, Dan. *Mary Todd Lincoln.* New York: Children's Press, 1999.

Schneller, Robert J. *A Quest for Glory; A Biography of Rear Admiral John A. Dahlgren.* Annapolis: Naval Institute Press, 1996.

Schultz, Duane. *The Dahlgren Affair.* New York: W.W. Norton & Co., 1998.

Shaw, Archer H., comp. and ed. *The Lincoln Encyclopedia.* New York: The MacMillan Company, 1950.

Sherman, George W. *A Narrative of War Time, 20th Connecticut Volunteer Infantry.* Lynbrook, N.Y.: New Era Press, 1917.

Silverstone, Paul H. *Warships of the Civil War Navies.* Annapolis, MD: Naval Institute Press, 1989.

Sparks, David S., ed. *Inside Lincoln's Army; The Diary of Marsena Rudolph Patrick.* New York: Thomas Yoseloff, 1964.

Styple, William, ed. *Writing and Fighting the Civil War.* Kearney, N.J.: Belle Grove Publishing Co, 2000.

Tarbell, Ida M. *The Life of Abraham Lincoln.* Vol. 2, New York: Lincoln Historical Soc. (1895) 1900.

Taylor, John M. *William Henry Seward at Washington.* New York: HarperCollins, 1991.

Time Life eds. *Voices of the Civil War; Fredericksburg.* Alexandria, VA: Time Life Books, 1997.

Warner, Ezra J. *Generals in Blue; Lives of the Union Commanders.* Baton Rouge: Louisiana State University Press, (1964) 1992.

Wert, Jeffry D. *The Sword of Lincoln; The Army of the Potomac.* New York: Simon & Schuster, 2005.

Winn, Ralph, comp. *A Concise Lincoln Dictionary; Thoughts and Statement.* New York: Philosophical Library, Inc., 1959.

ILLUSTRATION SOURCES

Century Magazine, *The Century War Book; The Famous History of the Civil War by the People who Actually Fought It.* Originally published 1894 (New York: Arno Press, 1978): 54.

Conner, Jane: 44.

Forbes, Edwin, *Army Sketch Book: Thirty Years After, an Artist's Story of the Great War.* (New York: Fords, Howard & Hulbert, 1890): 25.

Frank Leslie's Illustrated Newspaper, June 1, 1861: 3

Fredericksburg Area Museum: 13.

Fredericksburg and Spotsylvania National Military Park: 46.

Guernsey, Alfred H. and Henry M. Alden*, Harper's Pictorial History of the Civil War* (New York: The Fairfax Press, 1866): 79.

Harper's Weekly: 6, March 26, 1861 (U. Dahlgren), 55 & 56, May 2, 1863.

W. R. Kiefer, *History of the One Hundred & Fifty-third Regiment Penn. Volunteer Infantry,* (Easton, PA: The Chemical Publishing. Company, 1909): 65.

Library of Congress, Washington, D.C.: front cover, 4, 5, 6 (Field), 9, 10, 11, 14. 16, 17, 18, 19, 20, 21, 22, 23,27, 28, 30, 32, 34, 35, 36, 38, 39 (T. Lincoln), 40 (Bates), 41, 42,43, 45, 47, 48, 51 (Salm-Salm), 52, 53, 57, 60,61, 62, 63, 66,68, 73, 76, back cover.

National Archives, Washington, D.C.: 49.

Nimitz Library, U.S. Naval Academy, Annapolis: 7.

Richmond, Fredericksburg, and Potomac Railroad, William E. Griffin, Jr. Collection: 1, 2.

Russell, Andrew, *Russell's Civil War Photographs; 116 Historic Prints* (New York: Dover Publications, Inc., 1982): 33, 70.

Stackpole, Edward J., *Drama on the Rappahannock; The Fredericksburg Campaign,* (Harrisburg: The Stackpole Co., 1957): 24, 25, 31.

The National Bank of Fredericksburg: 45.

West Point Library, U.S. Military Academy, West Point, NY. Drawing by Durfee: 12.

Western Reserve Historical Society: 37.

White Oak Civil War Museum: 51 (Boscobel).

www.mrlincolnandfriends.org : 39 (Henry), 40 (Brooks)